Sculpting and handbuilding

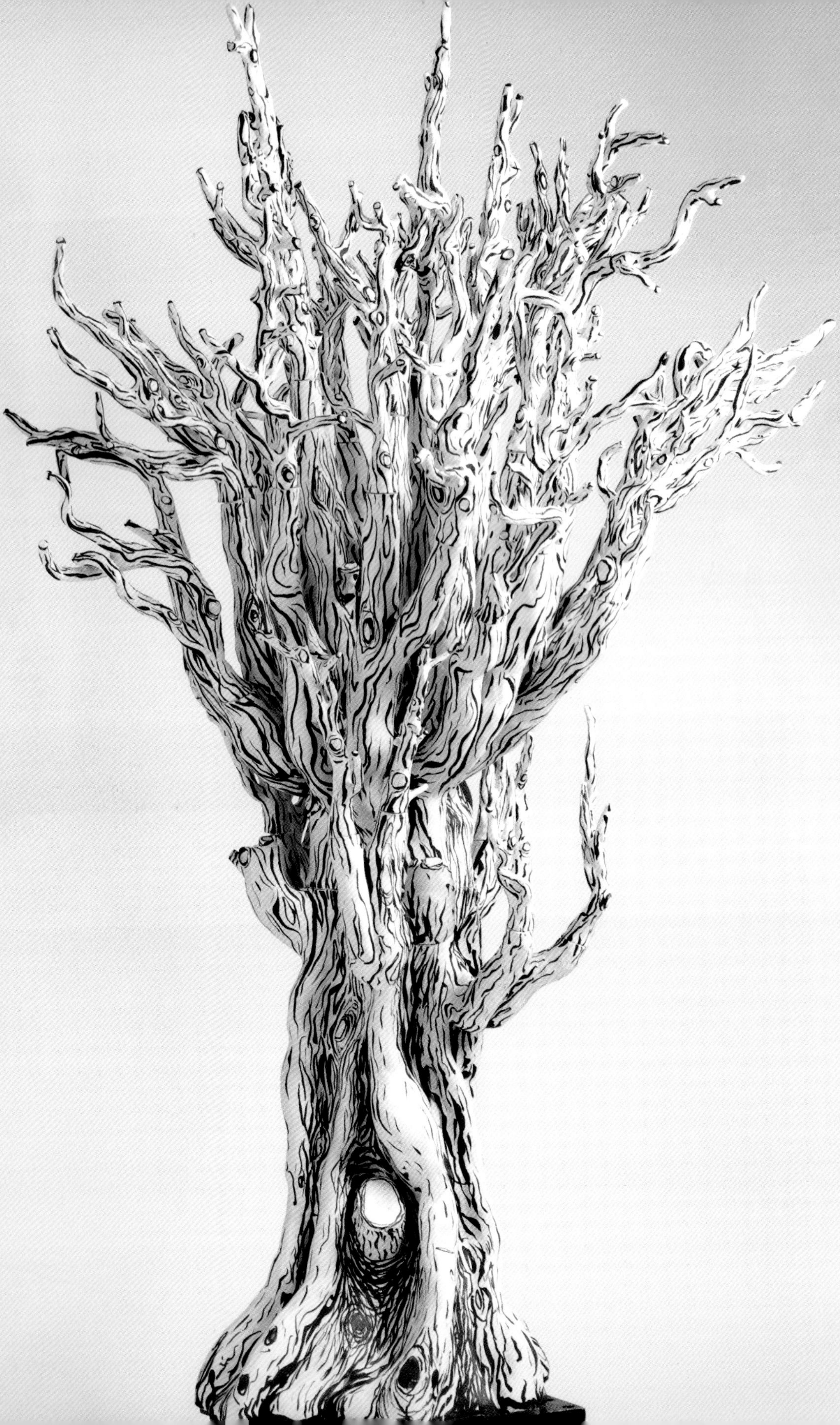

Sculpting and handbuilding

Claire Loder

The American Ceramic Society · Ohio

B L O O M S B U R Y
LONDON · NEW DELHI · NEW YORK · SYDNEY

Dedication
For John and Wren and all the miles walked to give me a quiet house.

First published in Great Britain in 2013
Bloomsbury Publishing Plc
50 Bedford Square
London WC1B 3DP
www.acblack.com

ISBN 978-1-4081-5668-1

Published simultaneously in the USA by
The American Ceramic Society
600 N. Cleveland Ave., Suite 210
Westerville, Ohio, 43082, USA
http://ceramicartsdaily.org

ISBN: 978-1-57498-334-0

Copyright © Claire Loder 2013

CIP Catalogue records for this book are available from the British Library.

All rights reserved. No part of this publication may be reproduced in any form or by any means – graphic, electronic or mechanical, including photocopying, recording, taping or information storage and retrieval systems – without the prior permission in writing of the publishers.

Claire Loder has asserted her right under the Copyright, Design and Patents Act 1988 to be identified as the author of this work.

Typeset in 10 on 13pt Rotis Semi Sans
Book design by Susan McIntyre
Cover design by Sutchinda Thompson

Printed and bound in China.

This book is produced using paper that is made from wood grown in managed, sustainable forests. It is natural, renewable and recyclable. The logging and manufacturing processes conform to the environmental regulations of the country of origin.

COVER IMAGES: Merete Rasmussen, *Blue Twisted Form* (detail), 2011. Stoneware, coiled, 40 x 60 x 60 cm (16 x 24 in). *Photo: courtesy of the artist.*
COVER IMAGES: Fenella Elms, *Green Flow* (detail), 2011. Stained porcelain, wall mounted, 60 x 55 cm (24 x 22 in). *Photo: courtesy of the artist.*

FRONTISPIECE: Katherine Morling, *Large Tree*. Crank clay and porcelain, porcelain slip and black stain, 2 x 1m (6½ x 3¼ft). Hand built and slab built. *Photo: courtesy of the artist.*

RIGHT: Manuel Canu, *Floor installation*, 2011. Detail. *Photo: Ole Akhøj.*

Contents

Acknowledgements   6

About the author   7

Introduction 9

   1 Handbuilding techniques 13

   2 Research and inspiration 47

   3 The vessel 63

   4 Surface treatments 77

   5 Sculptural approaches 87

   6 Combining techniques and materials 99

   7 Contemporary approaches 113

Conclusion   123

Featured Artists   124

Bibliography   125

Suppliers   126

Index   127

Acknowledgements

Writing this book has been a fascinating experience and I'm grateful to Alison Stace of Bloomsbury for giving me the opportunity to do it and to Kate Sherington for her considered guidance and encouragement as editor.

This has turned into a rewarding project, researching, connecting and communing with so many different artists, potters and ceramicists – some on my doorstep, others around the world. I've had the chance to talk to artists who inspired me when I was starting out, and others whose work I have delighted in discovering over the years.

This could so easily have been a much larger book. I had to (reluctantly) stop somewhere, which is testament to the quality and inventiveness of the work currently being produced. Thank you to all the artists who have so generously given me their time and supplied information and many wonderful images. Thanks to my family and friends for their support and encouragement, especially Mandy, Bek, Rob, Maki and Mum for their special efforts in getting me to this point. I realise now something about what went into the books that inspired me when I was starting out in ceramics. Thanks, John, for your hour upon hour of patient practical assistance and for helping me to find the space and time to do this in the midst of blurry-eyed first time parenthood, and for being the calm in my life. I've always wanted to say thank you somewhere and somehow to Val Cornish my A-level art teacher who inspired a confidence and commitment in me – she never taught me ceramics but she did instil in me an appreciation for so many things that have sustained my creative life. Last but not least, thanks to Susan for my room with a view.

Ruan Hoffmann, canopic-style jar (and detail of skull), 2012. Copper oxide, glass, glaze and lustre.
Photo: Mari Engelbreght.

About the author

I came to ceramics from painting and to painting from illustration. I still find myself painting and drawing, but now in ceramics, making touchable objects with materials that excite me more than acrylic and board ever did.

My creative life has always been about empirical exploration. This, combined with that fact that I'm an interloper in the world of ceramics, has made the writing of this book a curious experience. I want to say, 'do your own thing, explore, experiment', but I remember my own first fumblings with clay and the search for those little pieces of information that made the world of difference.

Having been on the receiving end of 'No, this is how it should be done', one time too many during my art education, I'm a firm advocate of open exploration. This is not to diminish the importance of discipline or the gaining of essential skills that lead to the making of remarkable work. It's more to do with embracing an open way of thinking rather than a prescriptive way of doing.

Hopefully this book is a balance of the tried and tested, with enough inspirational case studies and words of encouragement to motivate you to try your own thing.

Claire Loder, portrait with *What Do I Stand For?* 2009. Slab-built head, slip, underglazes, oxide, matt glaze, single-fired, height: 40 cm (15¾ in). *Photo: John Taylor.*

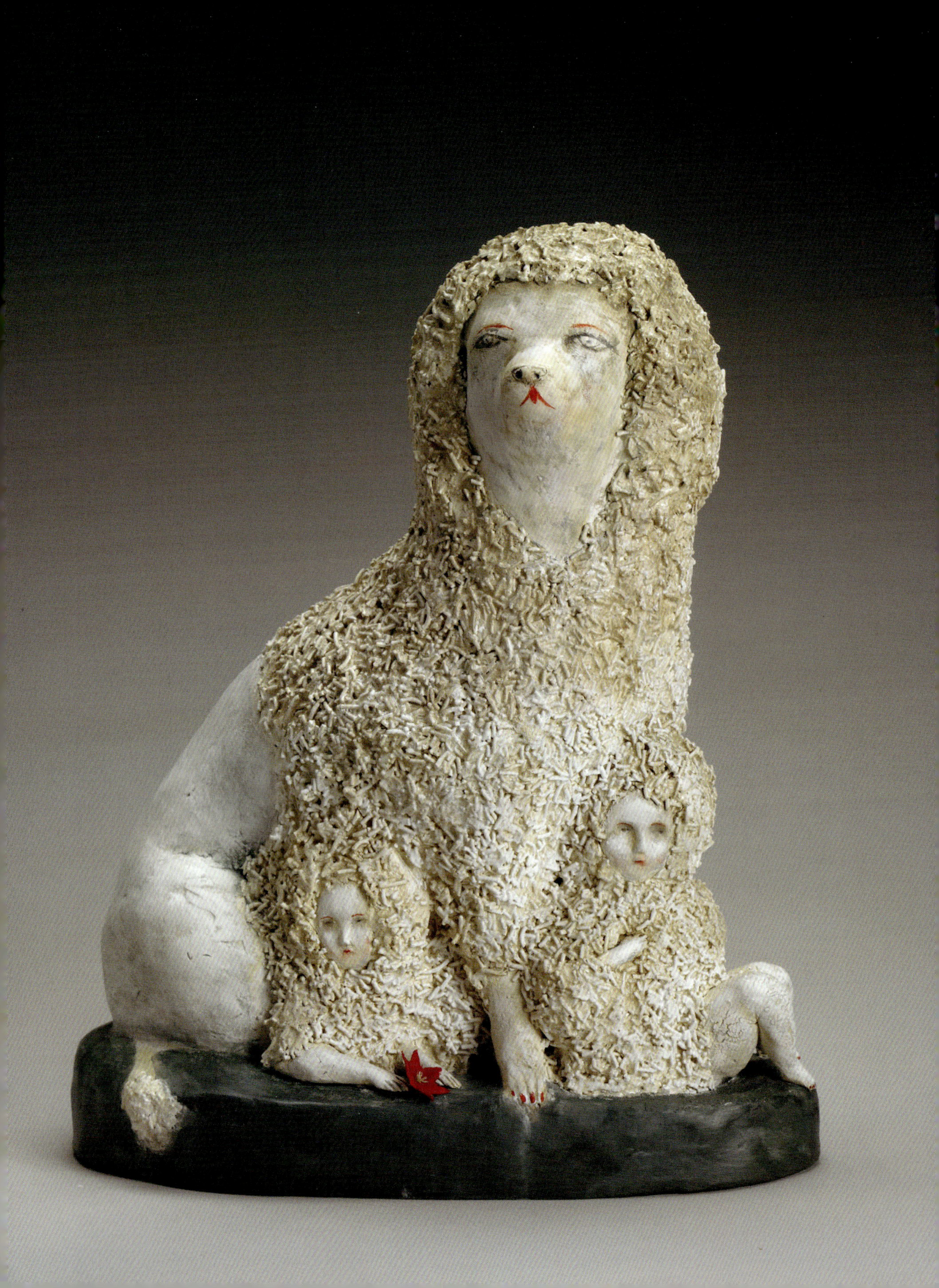

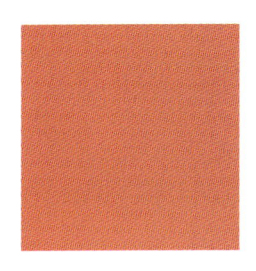

Introduction

'Clay invites us to make our mark, squeezing the soft clay between our hands and giving form to our ideas.'[1] Steve Mattison

Over the millennia, our species has coaxed practical, complex and beautiful objects from innocuous lumps of clay. It's no different today. The miraculous transformation of earth into object has great appeal for artists, and offers remarkable creative potential. The metamorphosis of the raw material of clay by the actions of our bare hands is arguably the most dramatic leap: a remarkable transformation carried out with the simplest of tools.

However complex the final piece is, it all starts with the elementary activity of manipulating a ball of clay in the palm of our hands. Handbuilding and sculpting is the simplest approach to clay: using this method, little equipment is needed to transform this responsive and engaging material.

Pots and figures were the first hand-formed clay objects. Ritual figures, often used in religious ceremonies, were modelled by hand. Before the invention of the potter's wheel, vessels were also made by pinching, coiling, slab-building or patting/beating out a shape from a lump of clay. These methods are unchanged today and are still employed across the globe.

Out of these humble beginnings and over centuries, trade, art and industry emerged. Industrial production and invention layered complexity upon this modest material. Now handbuilding is just one aspect of the multifarious field of ceramics. The vastness of the discipline and the traditions bound up in the production of ceramic objects, often a very technical and process-heavy pursuit, can be overwhelming and intimidating to newcomers. Putting aside the complexities of process and concentrating on the clay itself, forming by hand represents many possibilities for the novice and the established artist. There is nothing like the material experience of hands-on exploration and getting your hands dirty.

Today, the ceramics community as a whole retains and maintains a high level of skill and material knowledge, and ensures a continuum from the techniques of centuries past. Some within the community are complementing and challenging the conventional approaches by exploring new territories: working with raw clay, combining materials and developing new means of presentation. These practitioners bring expertise and insight from other disciplines, strengthening the link between clay and the wider creative industries.[2] Their new approaches sit happily and unhappily, to varying degrees, alongside the traditional ways.

This book explores the process and outcomes of handbuilding and sculpting, looking at the basic techniques and a selection of makers, artists and designers

LEFT: Bonnie Smith, *Watchdog*, 2011. Earthenware, glaze, paint, sculpted and coil-built, 33 x 28 cm (13 x 11 in). *Photo: Storm Photo.*

Sculpting and handbuilding

Kaori Tatebayashi, *Tennis Shoes*, 2006. White stoneware, slab-built. *Photo: courtesy of the artist.*

who employ, combine and subvert them. It is by no means a comprehensive survey, but more a springboard for further research by the reader. Coming originally from another discipline, I am at times overwhelmed by the vastness of the field of ceramics and the weight of tradition. For me, the complexities of process and all the creative expression they offer are separate from the physical experience of handling clay. As in thrall as we have been to the traditions and conventions of ceramics there is much to be said for the pure sensation of handling the clay in its delightfully responsive, original state.

Although I have chosen various makers to illustrate the subject of each chapter, each particular chapter by no means defines the artists it contains. Having the chance to talk to ceramic artists while compiling this book has, for me, further emphasised the variety of working methods, philosophies, attitudes and predilections of those working with clay. While there is often debate that the range of working practices is too disparate to unify ceramics as a subject, I consider this variety the life-blood of a dynamic field.

Notes
[1] Steve Mattison, *The Complete Potter*, Quarto Publishing, London, 2003.
[2] Duncan Hooson and Julia Rowntree, *Firing Up Handbook*, Crafts Council, 2010.

RIGHT: Claire Loder, *Losing my bloom*, 2009. White earthenware, slip, underglazes, matt glaze, single-fired, height: 64 cm (25 in). *Photo: John Taylor.*

Introduction

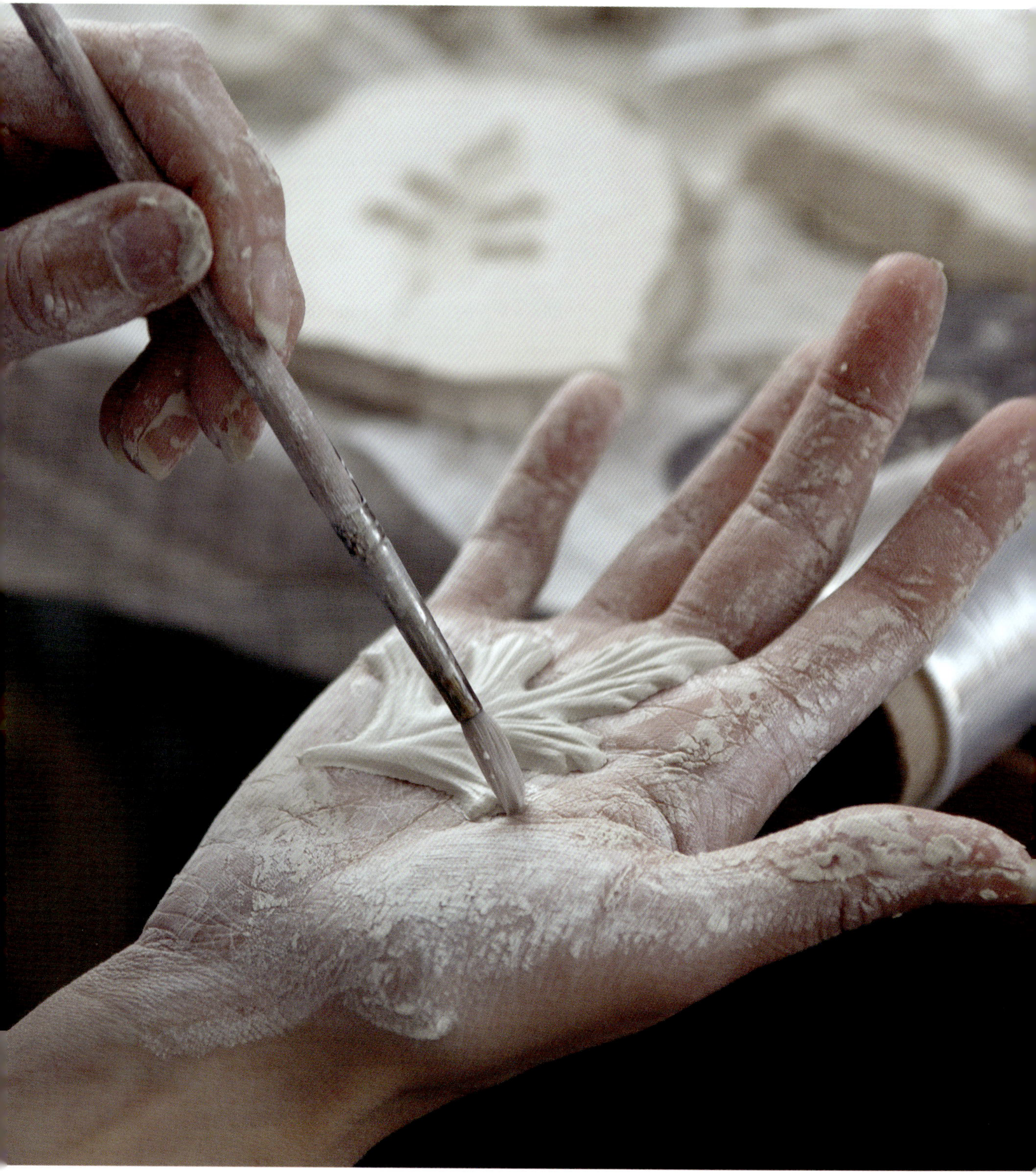

1 Handbuilding techniques

'Clay is egalitarian and playful ... it can be formed, pinched, pulled and sculpted.'[1]
Antony Quinn

Handbuilding is one of the most basic and versatile ways of making clay objects, the other two commonly used techniques being throwing and mould-making. Handbuilding offers artists great capacity for free expression and all the advantages of an intuitive approach.

The experience and knowledge to be gained by experimenting with the basic processes is significant. Understanding these processes will help you learn how the clay responds in your hands. For example, making a pinch pot helps you to understand the relationship between the initial ball size and the resulting object, while coiling and slab-building teach you how to scale up and enable you to work quickly. Carving and sculpting will hone your three-dimensional skills and give you a feel for the consistency of clay and its drying times.

All handbuilding techniques derive from a few simple processes: coiling, pinching, slab-building, carving and sculpting. Their definitions are amorphous and each process does not exist in isolation. Ceramicists, artists and potters combine, subvert and circumvent these processes to obtain the results they require. This chapter explores each of the techniques and offers tips on working with clay.

Preparing the clay

To minimise the risk of air bubbles, to ensure an even consistency and a decent, workable condition, it is good practice to prepare the clay before you begin working with it. Many ceramicists (including myself) use the manufacturer's clay straight from the bag without any trouble. Others always wedge their clay before they use it. It is important to understand how to eliminate pockets of air and produce workable clay whether you are using clay from the bag or not, especially as reclaiming or recycling clay should be a part of sustainable practice (see p. 16). It is also useful to understand what can happen if you don't fully prepare the clay, not only so you can diagnose problems that may occur in the firing, but also because you may want to capitalise on the cracks, splits and irregularities that arise as possible routes of investigation in your work, and to encourage these as features rather than flaws.

LEFT: Phoebe Cummings making porcelain sprig-moulded leaves in the residency studio at the Victoria and Albert Museum, London, 2010. Leaf designs were drawn from patterns printed and painted on tableware in the museum collection. These designs were then modelled by hand in clay, from which plaster sprig-moulds were created. Individual leaves were pressed from the moulds to build together into three-dimensional forms.

Wedging and kneading

Most ceramicists mix the clay by hand using various wedging and kneading techniques. Everyone has their favoured method and there is much debate about what works best. Confusingly, kneading is also referred to as wedging. Whatever their labels, there are two principal actions. One encourages consistency by aligning the clay particles and one works out any trapped air.

The first stage involves cutting a block of clay in half, rotating one half and slamming it down on top of the other. This promotes an even distribution of the clay molecules and any additives, such as grog. The second stage involves pushing down on the clay while working it into a spiral. This action eliminates any air pockets and evens out the moisture in the clay. Clay that already has an even consistency only needs the air expelling.

Wedging and kneading are physically-demanding activities, so it is important to work at the right height and maintain a comfortable working position. Get your body 'behind' the clay, so that you can use your body weight to help with the wedging. If you need to consistently prepare large amounts of clay, then a pugmill makes the job much easier. You will also need a strong workbench with an absorbent surface such as a plaster bat or canvas-covered board.

To expel any air from the clay it needs to be malleable. If the clay is too stiff, add water by poking your fingertips into the body of clay, filling the indentations with water and leaving it for a while.

There are various ways of spiralling the clay when wedging. Illustrated here is the 'ram's head' or 'ox head' technique.

How to wedge and knead

1. To wedge the clay, work on a firm, absorbent surface. Cut a block of clay in half with a wire, pick up the top piece, rotate it by 90 degrees and slam it down on the other half of the block. Repeat this process until the clay is mixed.

2. Before kneading, make sure the amount of clay you are preparing is easy for you to handle. Stand at your bench with your feet apart and one foot slightly in front of the other; use the weight of your body to rock the clay to and fro.

3. For the 'ram's head' technique, shape the clay into a rough rectangle and place your hands on opposite sides of the block. Tilt the clay up, cupping each side with your fingers, and then push down and away with the heel of your hands. The tilt and push action becomes a rocking movement which works the clay into a ram's heads shape

4. Cut the clay mass with a wire to check for air holes. If there are pockets of air visible, repeat the process, making sure to rotate the cut section and slam it down on the other half of the block as before.

Wedging is difficult to describe and takes practice to learn. If you are unable to find someone to show you how to do it in person, many online video tutorials are available, which are a good start. Try ceramicartsdaily.org, 'Clay wedging 101: A great way to teach and learn to wedge clay properly', or Youtube.com 'Pottery for beginners: wedging clay in pottery'.

Handbuilding techniques

Cutting the clay block for wedging using a cheese wire.

Slamming one half of the block down on the other.

'Ram's head' kneading – pushing the block down while cupping the outer edges.

Tilting the block up.

Pushing the block away from your body.

The 'ram's head' shape. *Photos: John Taylor.*

15

Sculpting and handbuilding

LEFT: Fenella Elms building one of her intricate structures. *Photo: David Parmiter.*

Reclaiming clay

It is very hard to avoid waste when you work with clay, but the good news is that until it is fired, all clay can be reclaimed and used again. Keep a lidded bucket, one for each type of clay (one for stoneware, one for terracotta, etc.) close at hand so you can collect all your scraps, trimmings, off-cuts and dried-out bits of clay as you go along.

How to reclaim clay

1. When you have a full bucket of scraps, lay all the clay pieces out on a clean, dry surface and allow them to dry out completely. If you break them into similar sizes, they will dry consistently.

2. Return the clay to the bucket and add water until it is completely immersed. Leave it for a few days to disintegrate or 'slake down' in the water. It will gradually turn into sludge. As the clay disintegrates, remove the excess water with a jug until only a small amount remains.

3. When you have removed as much excess water as possible, pour the soft mixture onto a plaster bat. Spread it out evenly to encourage consistent drying. Turn the mixture over regularly so that every part of the wet clay comes into contact with the bat.

4. When the clay has stiffened and is just dry enough to handle, roll it into a ball and remove it from the bat. Wedge it thoroughly, cutting through with the wire repeatedly. If the mass of clay is too large to handle in one go, break it down into smaller chunks. Knead the clay to give it consistency, then wrap and store.

Handbuilding techniques

ABOVE: Reclaiming clay: breaking the clay into small pieces to dry.

RIGHT: Covering clay with water.

RIGHT, BELOW: Spreading wet clay onto a plaster bat.
Photos: John Taylor.

Tools

The type of tools and equipment required depend on the kind of work you are making. Handbuilding, by its nature, relies on only a few essential tools, though there are some additional pieces of equipment that make working easier. Many potters and makers craft or adapt their own tools, especially tools for cutting or modelling, but you can easily buy the basics to get started.

A basic toolkit consists of a potter's knife for cutting the clay; a cheese wire to slice through the clay block; metal and rubber kidneys for scraping and smoothing; a rolling pin; modelling tools and a potter's needle. Materials for wrapping (such as newspaper and plastic sheeting or plastic bags), a water mister or spray and a sponge for cleaning your work-station are also essential.

Sculpting and handbuilding

There are a few other useful tools and pieces of equipment. A banding wheel enables you to access the form easily and maintain a comfortable working height. Wooden boards make transporting and storing work easier and are useful for laying drying slabs or reclaimed clay on. A plaster bat is really useful for clay preparation and reclamation; a piece of canvas stretched across your table or fastened to a board works just as well. A selection of containers of various sizes, including bowls and buckets, is always handy, as is a small lidded pot for storing slip used for joining. A selection of brushes, spatulas and modelling tools can be bought, adapted or made.

LEFT: Tools and equipment – banding wheel, potter's knife, potter's needle, metal kidney, cheese wire, rolling pin, wooden modelling tools (in pot), rubber kidney (being used). At the back: water mister, selection of brushes, wooden spatulas and spoons.

BELOW: Various-sized loop tools used for carving.

BELOW LEFT: Examples of Frankie Locke's handmade or appropriated carving tools, and metal kidneys. *Photos: John Taylor.*

Christy Keeny, *The Bull*, 2010. Flax clay, painted with red earthenware slip and finished with oxides – manganese dioxide and copper oxide, 34 x 26 cm x 12 cm (13½ x 10¼ x 4¾ in). *Photo: courtesy of the artist.*

The techniques

Pinching

Pinching a pot from a ball of clay is often our first experience of handling the material. This rudimentary method works with all types of clay and is remarkably versatile. Pinching is the technique that carries the mark of the maker most visibly. Ceramicists such as Ingrid Bathe and Lilly Zuckerman exploit this characteristic, and their forms retain the traces of their making. The repetitive motion of their fingertips pinching the clay is evident in the surface of their work to varying degrees. This elementary technique can result in sophisticated and sensitive forms.

Pinching usually starts with a ball of clay sitting in the palm of your hand. Because the clay dries quickly from the warmth of your hands, pinching works best with soft clay. The drier the clay, the more risk of cracking and crumbling. This technique is a great way to learn about how clay responds to your touch.

A pinched pot can be manipulated or adapted into many shapes. Pinching is also a way of building up a form in combination with other processes. For example, you may have a slab-built base to which you add a pinch pot – or you can add bands of clay that you then pinch out.

Sculpting and handbuilding

How to make a pinch pot and a hollow form

1. Start with a ball of clay that comfortably sits in your hand. Mould it into a sphere. Supporting the sphere with one hand, press the thumb of your other hand into the centre of the ball. This basic principle of supporting one side of the clay while manipulating the other is the same across all the processes described here.

2. While keeping your thumb in place, rotate the clay around it. Begin at the bottom of the hole and pinch the clay between your forefinger and thumb. This action will expand the walls and also create the base of the pot. Squeeze the clay between your thumb and forefinger to judge the thickness of the base.

3. Once you have the basic shape, continue rotating the pot and squeezing out the base, walls and finally the rim until you have the thickness you require. Always leave the rim until last to avoid it cracking. Any cracks that appear can be smoothed with a finger or cut off with a knife.

From this basic method, a variety of pinch pots can be made. By altering the shape and depth of the initial hole and the amount of pressure and pulling you use to expand the walls, you can make many different shapes. Rolling the ball into a cone before pinching will produce an elongated form. Gently pulling the walls from the inside using your fingertips while supporting the outside wall will coax the form outwards. To shape the walls inwards, fold, gather or make a v-shaped cut and rejoin the edges.

4. A useful shape to make from a pinch pot is a hollow sphere. Made from two pinched sections joined together, this form can be adapted to make figurative forms, boxes and other hollow objects. After preparing two pots, cross-hatch the edge of each and wet with slip. Press together.

5. Firmly seal the join with your fingertips. A thorough join will ensure that the air captured in the hollow remains intact. The air pressure acts as a support, keeping the form inflated while you work on it. Once sealed, the object can be squeezed, rolled or paddled. Fix any punctures or cracks that appear with soft clay. Once you have finalised the form, and before the sphere dries out, make a small hole in it with a potter's needle, allowing enough air to escape and thus preventing cracks as your object dries and shrinks.

RIGHT: How to make a pinch pot and a hollow form. *Photos: John Taylor.*

Lilly Zuckerman makes pinched earthenware vessels. She explains her process: 'Starting with a solid block of clay, I slowly and methodically pinch the form. No clay is added and very little clay is trimmed away ... encompassing many changes of state, from the uncomplicated lump, heavy with potential, through precarious and fluid chaos, and ending with the form.'

A trip to Morocco, where the adobe buildings, cooking pots and geology inspired her forms, left Zuckerman with the sensation of seesawing between vast open countryside and claustrophobic narrow streets, zooming in and out from one vista to another. The presentation of her pinched vessels on vast farmhouse tables captures something of this sensation (see p. 118). Viewed from afar, as a horizontal panorama, the collection of vessels appears as clustered dwellings across the fields. Close up, they resemble buildings, walls, courtyards and alleyways.

Handbuilding techniques

Sculpting and handbuilding

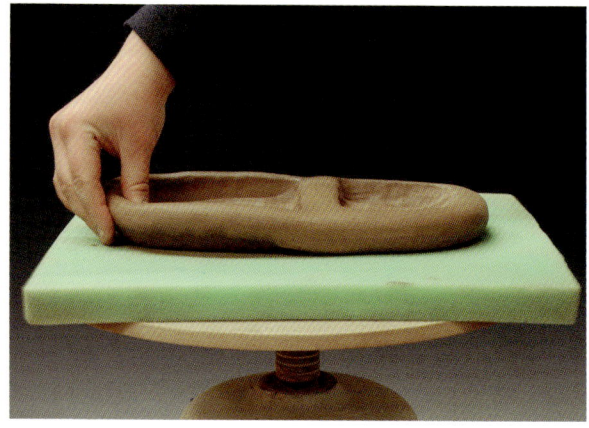

ABOVE, LEFT: Lilly Zuckerman, initial stages of forming a vessel with her fingertips from a thick clay slab.

ABOVE, RIGHT: Lilly Zuckerman, pinching out the two chambers of the tray.

LEFT: Lilly Zuckerman, coaxing the clay upwards, refining the walls. *Photos: Lilly Zuckerman.*

BELOW: Lilly Zuckerman, *Earthenware Tray*, 2011. Dimensions: 38 x 30 x 10 cm (15 x 12 x 4 in). *Photo: Lilly Zuckerman.*

Coiling

Coiling involves creating and using lengths or ropes of clay to build up a form. Endlessly versatile, coils can be used to build quickly and expressively. It is an ideal method for making large-scale work, but it can also be used to build fine, delicate objects. As Betty Blandino beautifully describes, coils 'may be as regular as bricks layered to build a wall, as random as dry stonewalling, or as rhythmical as knitting. They may give the pot the quality of the geological stratification of a cliff face, the wispy structure of a bird's nest, or the organic crumble of the earth's crust – or they may be smoothed to make the surface indistinguishable from that of pots made by other methods'.[2]

Coils are formed from lumps of clay rolled on an absorbent surface using the palms of the hands. A heavily-grogged clay can be squeezed in the hand to make a rough rope-like shape, then refined by rolling it on the work surface. Coils can be as small or as large as your hands will allow. Smaller coils are suited to fine small-scale pieces, while larger coils are good for building larger pieces and quicker building. A fine clay, like porcelain, is good for delicate coils that make thin-walled vessels. But there is nothing to stop a counterintuitive approach: try rough, quickly-formed coils and see how the porcelain responds. As for the shape of the coils themselves, they can be long ropes or short pellets depending on the nature of the form you are constructing.

Depending on the type of clay and the size of the coils used, coiling can be a fast process, ideal for building intuitively or with precision, which skilfully mimics other processes, such as casting or throwing. Grogged clay, such as crank or raku clay, formed into fat coils, is ideal for building fast and expressively. At the other end of the scale, porcelain is finer and results in a more subtle, refined structure.

Like all handbuilding processes, coiling is easily combined with other techniques. For example, composite objects can be constructed by joining a coiled organic shape to an angular, rigid slab form. Or fine coils can be added piece by piece to a rough-hewn lump of clay. Throwers often complete their forms with coiled sections. A coil can even become slab-like by flattening a rolled coil to make a ribbon of clay.

Coiling tips

Allow for drying time as you build, especially with large structures. Coils already in place will need to be stiff enough to support subsequent coils built up on top and avoid collapse. Air-dry your form; the most recent coils can be wrapped in plastic to preserve moisture while allowing the lower coils to stiffen. If you are varying the thickness of the coils, or combining processes, then drying times become even more important. In these cases it is essential to dry the work slowly to prevent cracks appearing at the stress points between thick and thin sections of clay.

Fresh clay will be soft enough for each coil to adhere to the next without adding slip. If the top coil becomes too dry, then score the surface and brush it with slip before adding the next coil. The coils need to be firmly joined on the inside of the form to prevent horizontal cracks.

Coiling is a particularly adaptable way to build. To adjust the form you can manipulate the coils with your fingers by squeezing or pulling them, or paddle the clay into shape with the appropriate tool, as illustrated in the pinch-pot section. For a small pot you can build with one continuous coil in an upwards spiral. For larger pieces, you can prepare the coils and store them in plastic. For fast building you can use an extruder tool, which has a shaped die plate at one end. This allows you to create different coil profiles depending on the aperture of the die plate.

RIGHT: Coiling a vessel shape. *Photos: John Taylor.*

Coiling a vessel shape

1. Working on an absorbent surface such as a plaster bat or canvas, create a clay slab by using a rolling pin or the palm of your hand. Cut out the base of your piece. Alternatively you could start with a pinch pot, or coil the base, starting from the centre and coiling outwards in a spiral. This can be done flat or by rolling a coil on its side.

2. From sections of prepared (wedged/kneaded) clay, roll out coils using the palms of your hands and your fingers. Start with your hands close together and move them wider apart to lengthen the coil. Rotating the coil will keep it round and prevent it from flattening too much. As you build, the coils will thin out, so make them slightly thicker than the required width of the final wall.

3. Working with a board or bat on a banding wheel, add the first coil to the base. If the clay is soft enough it will bond without water. If the coils are drier you will need to score the surface of the bottom coil and add slip before attaching the new coil.

4. With a dragging motion, using your finger or a tool, attach the first coil to the base along the inside edge. Where the ends of the coil meet, smooth the clay together. As you build, stagger these joins to avoid creating a vertical stress point.

5. Once you have several coils in place, bond them together from the inside whilst supporting the clay on the outside. Do this by dragging the clay downwards with the tip of your finger. If required, smooth the interior surface with a wooden tool. You can join the coils on the outside too (as shown here) or leave them intact.

6. If you are building a form that opens out, as shown here, make each new coil slightly larger in diameter. Do the reverse to taper in. Consider your surface: for a totally smooth finish, bond the coils as in Step 5, then smooth and refine with a metal kidney. This surface has been textured by using fingers to blend the clay downwards in a rhythmic motion.

Danish ceramicist **Merete Rasmussen**'s abstract sculptural forms explore the possibilities of a continuous surface. Soft curves contrast with sharp edges, concave shifts to convex, and negative spaces and inner space oscillate. With no visible start or end, these wide ribbons of undulating clay are purposefully perplexing for the viewer and technically challenging for the artist. Rasmussen uses stoneware clay and, incredibly, her pieces are coil-built. 'I like to challenge the material and my own skills by building complicated shapes,' she says, 'fragile in the building, drying and firing

Handbuilding techniques

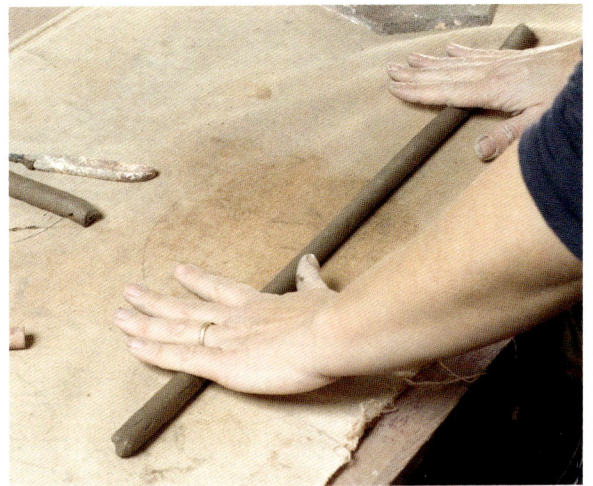

process, which upon firing attain the strength to be handled and positioned without support.' These forms are both simple and complex and demonstrate Rasmussen's virtuosity for coiling. Her choice of strong matt colour for the surface emphasises the form and leads the eye repeatedly around the structure.

RIGHT: Merete Rasmussen, *Yellow Multi Loop*, 2011. Stoneware, coiled, 55 x 50 x 55 cm (21½ x 19½ x 21½ in). *Photo: Merete Rasmussen.*

Slab-building

This technique uses flat slabs of clay, shaped and joined to construct an object. Slab-building today owes much to the post-war sculptor-potters, whose innovative use of the technique formed part of their wider explorations into handbuilding. Coming to prominence in the 1960s, potters such as Ruth Duckworth, Gillian Lowndes, Gordon Baldwin and Ian Auld experimented with sculptural slab-built forms, demonstrating the versatility of the technique.

Slabs are pliable and fast to work with. They can be formed in numerous ways depending on the requirements of the maker. Slabs can be combined with coiling, throwing, pinching and many other forming techniques. They can be manipulated throughout the process of building but as the clay stiffens, options for manipulation lessen.

Slabs can be used in their leatherhard state to produce geometric, angular, architectural constructions and in their soft state to make organic, flowing forms. Soft-slabs are responsive to manipulation, touch and texture: they can be wrapped, draped, impressed, moulded, punctured, pulled and coaxed. Leatherhard slabs can form precise, complex, many-faceted objects, or the simplest, most exacting forms.

Making a slab

The method for producing a slab for building will depend on various factors including scale, surface requirements and building method. For large-scale slab-building, you may want to roll a slab on a large surface or use a slab roller tool. For a textured surface, you could roll a slab, then impress it with natural objects (bark, leaves, pine cones), or roll it over a carved plaster bat to create an impression in the slab. If you are building an object with many facets, a series of small slabs could be rolled out at once, or a template used to cut each facet from one large slab. The rolling pin is the most common tool, but anything that flattens or pushes the clay out will work just as well.

For an intuitive, asymmetric shape, start with a lump of clay and, working on an absorbent surface, form the slab with the heel of your hand, pushing down and away from you. Alternatively, flatten large lumps of clay by beating them with your fist or a mallet. If you start with a rudimentary method like this to form your slab then a smooth surface can always be achieved using a rolling pin.

For a more controlled approach and a neater slab, use a wire harp to slice slabs from a block. The most common method is to use a rolling pin and two wooden guides of equal thickness. Roll out the clay between the guides, remembering to rotate the slab by 90 degrees after every roll. You can make large slabs in this way as long as you have a large enough absorbent surface. For larger slabs without the effort, invest in a slab roller.

Handbuilding techniques

ABOVE, LEFT: James Oughtibridge refining a leatherhard form using a metal kidney.

ABOVE, RIGHT: James Oughtibridge, making a slab with a slab roller – here the clay is passing through the rollers.
Photos: Emma Oughtibridge.

Leatherhard slab construction

Leatherhard clay is characterised by its hard, cheese-like state; it is cold and firm to the touch. Leatherhard clay can still be effectively joined to softer clay using the cross-hatching and slip technique (see pictures opposite). Construction in this state is suited to the creation of angular, geometric, architectural forms.

Leatherhard clay allows for precise building. It can be cut without the clay dragging, so a more accurate cut can be achieved. Leatherhard slabs can also support their own weight. A template is useful if you are constructing an especially precise piece, as can cutting the slabs with a ruler. Slabs can be made and dried as you go along or you can roll out, dry, cut and store them in batches. Working with templates to construct forms from slabs is similar to pattern cutting, or constructing with cardboard. This can be a helpful comparison if you are a two-dimensional artist working with clay for the first time.

Making a slab box

1. Once you have rolled out your slabs, let them stiffen to a leatherhard state. This means clean cuts can be made in the clay and allow for more accurate construction. Softer clay will drag and burr as you cut it, making the slabs irregular and ragged.

2. Cross-hatch the edges to be joined and brush slip onto both sides. It is important this is done thoroughly for leatherhard clay. If you are working with softer slabs then dampening the edges with a wet brush or sponge will work.

3. Firmly press the wet edges together and slide the slab into place gently, forcing the liquid slip out from the joint and bonding the two pieces.

4. To reinforce the joint, roll out a thin coil and with your forefinger or a wooden modelling tool, press the coil into the joint. This prevents cracks by sealing the join firmly and distributing any pressure away from it.

5. Continue this method with the sides and base of the box, reinforcing each join with a coil. Once constructed, you can smooth the edges and surface of the box with a metal kidney.

RIGHT: Making a slab box.
Photos: John Taylor.

Handbuilding techniques

Sculpting and handbuilding

Soft-slab construction

Building with wet or soft slabs is suited (but not exclusive) to the creation of flowing, organic, intuitive, sculptural objects. If you are working with large slabs the clay needs to be dry enough to avoid tearing as you handle it, but wet enough to respond to the manipulations you will put it through. The room temperature will affect how fast your slabs dry out, as will your working speed. Wet clay can be thrown or slammed onto a surface to create an irregular-shaped slab of varying thickness, ideal for an asymmetric organic form.

Illustrated here is the author drawing and modelling her subject on the flat slab, then joining and constructing the head.

Claire Loder, slab-building a head – drawing the subject.

Stuffing with newspaper to support and shape the piece while it dries. *Photos: John Taylor.*

Handbuilding techniques

Cross-hatching the edges to be joined.

Joining the edges with wooden tool.

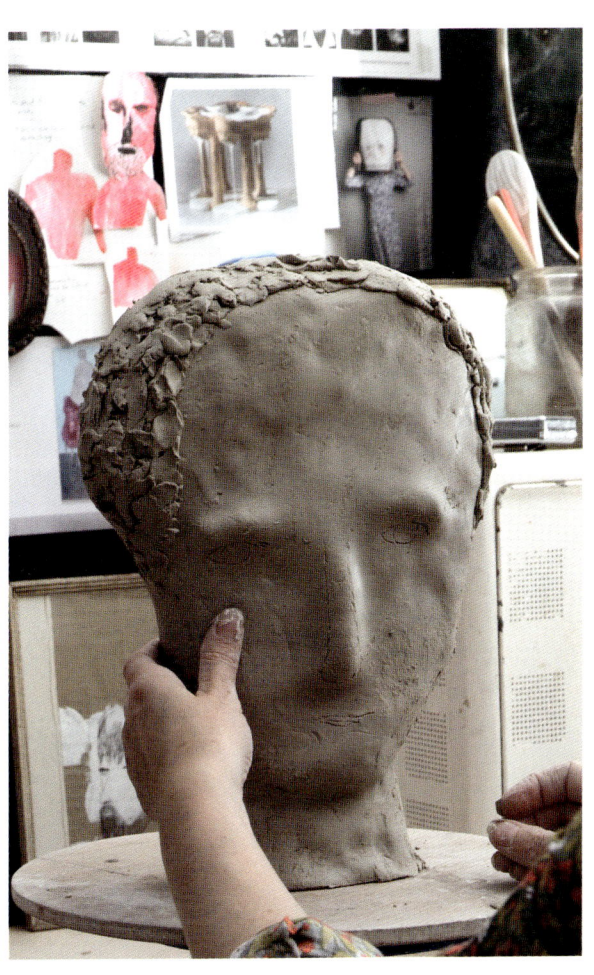

Refining the head once it can stand. *Photos: John Taylor.*

Moulds

Wet slabs can be moulded around a former. For example, a rolling pin is perfect for making a cylinder. Cover the rolling pin with newspaper to prevent the clay sticking to it and roll the slab around it, joining the clay where it overlaps by smoothing with your fingertips.

Slabs can be rolled out on a textured surface to pick up the imprint of that surface; they can be pressed into or onto anything to mould them into shape. You can drape a slab over a plate, press it into your cupped hand, or coax it into the peaks and troughs of a radiator. The options are limited only by your imagination.

Many artists make simple press-moulds out of plaster to form their pieces. James Oughtibridge (see p. 33) constructs his work in sections, each slab component being formed by laying it in a shallow mould overnight.

Sculpting and handbuilding

FAR LEFT: James Oughtibridge, draping a slab into a plaster mould. *Photo: Emma Oughtibridge.*

LEFT: Using the earth as a former. *Photo: John Taylor.*

A simple former is the earth itself, as used by ancient potters in the absence of other resources. A hollow is dug in the ground and clay pressed against the sides, making a vessel shape. It is then left until the clay form stiffens enough to be removed.

Slab-building tips

For sharp edges and crisp lines, work with leatherhard slabs. If the piece is complex you will need to plan ahead. Either prepare all your slabs before you start so that you have a ready supply or make sure that you have plenty of wrapping material (such as plastic sheets and/or damp cloths) to wrap up the piece between stages.

Make sure all edges are securely joined to reduce stress points. Thoroughly cross-hatch, slip and join, and if the piece is large, add a sausage of clay inside and out to further bond the sections of clay.

Newspaper is useful when slab-building: to ensure the even drying of your slabs, cover both sides of the slab with newspaper and flatten under a board. If you are using a former such as a rolling pin, block of wood or bowl, cover it with newspaper before applying the slab. To support or fill structures, scrunch newspaper up, lightly mist with water and stuff into the form.

The clay can be thick when you build, but an even thickness will result in consistent drying. This reduces any pressure on the joins as the piece dries, and during firing. Structures with thick walls will need longer to dry. Also remember that you will be lifting your work in and out of the kiln, so it must be strong enough to handle, and you will need to be strong enough to lift it!

James Oughtibridge, *Large Egg Shell Blue Vessel*, 2011. White underglaze and blue stain, 80 x 40 cm (31½ x 15¾ in). *Photo: Yvonne Grist.*

There is often wastage of clay with the slab-building technique, especially if you are using templates. If you are using soft-slabs, you can roll out what you need, cut out your shape and store the excess in a sealed bag for later use. With leatherhard slabs the clay will need to be reclaimed (see p. 16–17).

James Oughtibridge makes flowing sculptural forms that reference the vessel. His pieces are constructed using large slabs of clay, which are formed overnight in plaster moulds, until they retain the required curved shape. Initially James' sculptures take shape on the clay slabs. He draws flowing lines on the clay surface to work out where to cut away or add a section. His sculptures evolve through a process of cutting and reassembling. The finished pieces have numerous planes and perspectives, encouraging the play of light and shadow. His sculptures often appear to float, with no flat base visible.

Sculpting and handbuilding

Oughtibridge spends hours refining his surfaces, using surform tools (resembling graters) then kidneys and, once biscuit-fired, diamond pads of various grades. He works on the sculptures until the edges are crisp, and the surface itself is made smoother while still retaining a bit of texture from the sanding and scraping. Layers of underglaze, stains and oxides are applied and the pieces are fired to 1240°C (2264°F). The pale pieces are sealed with beeswax.

Jenny Southam's sculptures consist of several components. Southam fabricates each element using various handbuilding methods, then attaches each of the elements to the plinth. The plinth or base sets the stage for Southam's characters and objects, and allows a flexible approach to composition. Various combinations can be experimented with before the pieces are permanently attached to the base. To ensure a good join every surface is cross-hatched and slip is applied.

TOP: Jenny Southam fabricating the different components by hand modelling.

LEFT: Jenny Southam cross-hatching and dampening the surfaces to be joined to ensure a good join.
Photos: Kate & Josie Southam.

Carving

Carving, a currently underused technique, starts with a solid block of clay from which the artist carves a form. Working in this way maintains the traditions of carving with material such as wood or stone, but clay has the advantage of a more malleable surface that can be worked at various states of drying. Carving can be the trickiest technique to master, especially if you are new to clay. In terms of creative techniques, it can be a particularly expressive way to work, but carving depends on learning how to make work that will fire without cracking or exploding in the kiln. Judging the thickness and evenness of the carved walls is a skill you will need to develop and you must pay strict attention to drying times and fire work slowly up to 600°C/1112°F (see p. 45): the larger the scale of work the more critical these concerns become so it's a good idea to start with smaller objects and record all your results as you go along.

There are some objects that can only be created by carving. Building a form with deep indentations and complex patterns in the surface can be done with slab-building but it is a painstaking process; traditionally such forms have been carved in clay and cast. A solid block of clay is self-supporting and it is less complicated to subtract matter than to conceive a way of constructing one plane at a time.

Currently, relatively few ceramic artists choose to carve, maybe because so much of the history of ceramics is tied up with the vessel, a form so easily created by coiling, pinching and slabbing and clearly focused on hollow forms. It could also be because the other major tradition, of modelling in clay for casting purposes, is somehow the preserve of sculptors who work in other mediums and has yet to be fully taken up by the ceramics community.

Another reason could be that the immediacy of a pinch pot or slabbed box stands in stark contrast to the commitment of a carved object. There are particular difficulties when firing solid lumps of clay, but as with most issues, these can be sorted out by paying strict attention to drying times (and from practice and experience). Pieces may need to be dried for months, rather than weeks or days.

Although carving from a solid block is at present a neglected process, there are various carving techniques that have long been part of the ceramics canon, albeit applied largely to slabs of clay and thrown ware. Techniques like sgraffito, incising, and low- and high-relief carving are common. Carving from a block, like all handbuilding techniques, does not always happen in isolation and can be combined with other techniques and processes. Carving and sculpting are natural companions, the requirement to add and subtract clay matter being a customary part of an intuitive construction process.

Carving is usually associated with the exacting application of tools, but not all carved pieces are geometric or precise – an expressive, carved object can be formed with the fingers alone. Carving offers great scope for making your own tools, or appropriating other tools such as kitchen utensils and dentist's tools.

Carving tips

- Work out the design on the surface of the clay using a potter's needle to sketch what goes where. Alternatively, use paper templates, or transfer a design onto the clay by placing the paper design on the clay surface and pin-pricking the lines.
- If you are removing sections of clay to create negative spaces, use a loop tool to remove the main body, then a finer tool to perfect the carved shape.
- Throughout the process it's important to keep your tools clean, as this will ensure a clean cut and an accurate line.
- The wetness of the clay will have an impact on your carving. Wet clay offers less resistance, but may buckle when you remove clay, depending on your design. If the clay is too dry then it will become brittle and chip as you work on it.
- If you are working on a large piece, cover the areas not being worked and keep them moist. Carving creates all manner of stresses: different thicknesses, clay consistency and moisture levels all play a part, so wrap your work well and dry very slowly.
- Choose suitable clay for the piece you are working on. A large piece will require open and grogged clay, but smaller works can be made from finer clays. If you are interested in encouraging cracks, chips and stresses as part of your work then experiment with mixing clays. Clays that dramatically contrast, such as porcelain and crank, will produce the most marked results.
- In the early stages of experimentation, fire works in a saggar (see p. 44).

LEFT: Frankie Locke using a cheese wire to carve a block of laminated clay. *Photo: John Taylor.*

RIGHT: Frankie Locke using a handmade tool to carve a block of laminated clay. *Photo: John Taylor.*

Frankie Locke was brought up near the coast in South Wales and still lives and works in the area. Her laminated carved sculptures allude to the 'tumbling tides, pebbles, popples and rock pools' of her environment. Locke works from a solid block made up of laminated or layered coloured clays. She carves with a variety of tools, some found, some handmade. The technique of carving allows her to reveal the layered colours and patterns created during the formation of the block.

Locke has an MA in ceramics from UWIC in Cardiff. Before this, she studied Fine Art in Birmingham, and continues to work on both strands concurrently, one method and material feeding the other. All elements of Locke's work are tied together by her fascination with movement, fluidity of surface and form. These sculptures take

Frankie Locke, *Swell* (detail), 2010. Earthenware, 17 x 29 x 26 cm (6¾ x 11½ x 10¼ in). Photo: John Taylor.

considerable time to make and Locke is methodical in her colouring, layering, carving and drying, allowing her sculptures to dry for months before being fired. Her subject matter is transitory but her sculptures are indelible.

Jonathan Cross creates work that references geological formations and is infused with notions of the architectural and technological. His work also holds traces of his other interests, including minimalism, science fiction and Japanese wood-fired pottery. Typically he starts with a block of clay that he carves out during various stages of drying. He describes his work: 'By sculpting forms using a variety of techniques – cutting, tearing, chiselling, and carving – the work takes on this geological or natural quality. Using different clays, glazes and firing processes, the surfaces of the vessels are given a worn quality and patina, reinforcing the natural, aged look of the piece, evident in the earthy tones found on the vessels: dark basalt blacks, warm rust reds and sandy oranges.'

Jonathan Cross, *Axis Fault*, 2011. Carved black stoneware, soda-fired, 15 x 28 x 10 cm (6 x 11 x 4 in). Photo: Darren Looker.

Sculpting

Sculpting is loosely defined by the building up of clay, rather than subtraction. This is a highly expressive way of working and at its most basic relies solely on the hands as tools. The term is used to define a huge working range, from intricate and intimate processes to a whole body experience. Sculptures in clay vary greatly in scale and style: from figurines delicately modelled with the thumb and forefinger in the palm of the artist's hand, to vigorous works produced by hurling wet clay at a structure to build up form, and everything in between. Sculpting with clay can be fast and immediate, suited to large-scale pieces and outdoor works. It can also be small and expressive, conjuring up images of the first figures of ancient times, whose features were squeezed out of wet clay to resemble animals and human forms. Sculpting utilises the plasticity of clay.

Sculpting tips

- Any clay can be sculpted. Grogged clay is better at supporting itself and ideal for large sculptures, while finer clays are good for small-scale work. It is worth experimenting with different clays, as sculpting is often a highly tactile experience; the physical qualities of one clay may suit you more than those of another.
- Sculpting with clay often involves supporting the structure as it is created. Depending on the scale, form and composition of the piece, there are various methods of doing this. Small-scale pieces can be supported with scrunched up newspaper, pieces of sponge, or sticks with clay applied to each end. Building directly onto the kiln shelf, using kiln props to support appendages, makes transferring the piece to the kiln easier. Larger pieces can be supported by constructing internal walls and structures as you build.
- A metal framework or armature is often used to support large, complex objects. Armature wire is commonly used, in combination with chicken wire and wooden struts. Artists develop their own methods depending on the requirements of their work.
- **Be aware** that any non-ceramic materials that go into the kiln as part of your ceramic works, internal supports or other additives, and which burn away during the firing, may result in harmful fumes. Adequate ventilation is vital for all firings and ideally extraction fans should be fitted.

Susan O'Byrne builds large-scale ceramic animals from a patchwork of clay slabs. O'Byrne was born in Cork, Ireland. She now works from a Glasgow studio where she produces sculptural works, using the animal form as a vehicle for the expression of human emotions. She is interested in the use of animals in storytelling, legend and folklore throughout history, to simplify the complexities of adult life. 'I aim to give my animals a certain awkward vulnerability. This is achieved through a very personal making process. I make a wire framework, onto which layers of printed and patterned pieces of porcelain paperclay are applied to form a skin. The natural twists and kinks of the wire frame and the shrinkage of the clay around it during firing are allowed to dictate the posture of the finished animal. The element of chance in these processes is central to my work.'

FACING PAGE, TOP LEFT: Susan O'Byrne's nichrome wire armature covered in paper rods and hung from scaffolding. Paperclay tube legs are attached to the armature.

TOP RIGHT: Susan O'Byrne's nichrome wire armature covered with thin layers of paperclay.

BOTTOM: Susan O'Byrne, *Goat*, 2012. Porcelain paperclay, 115 x 100 x 35 cm (45¼ x 43¼ x 13¾ in). *Photos: courtesy of the artist.*

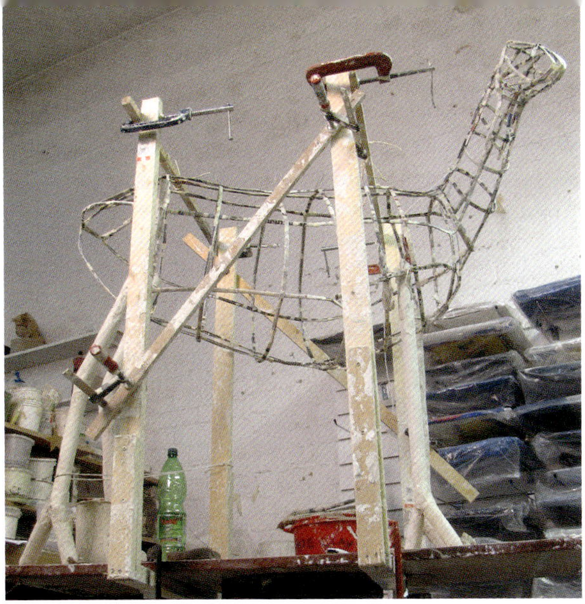
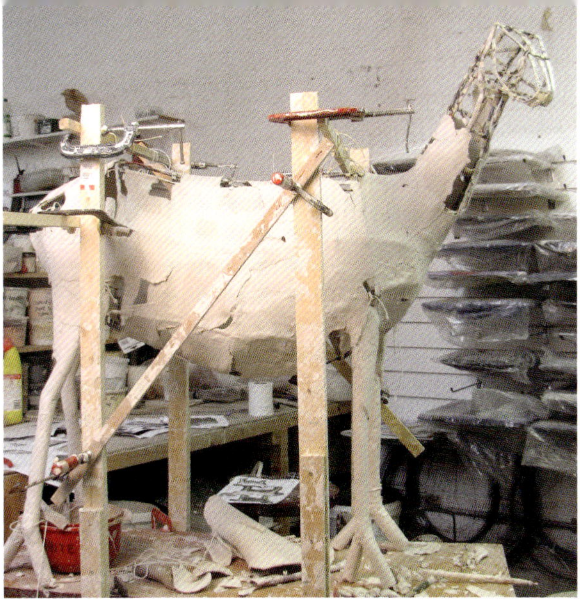
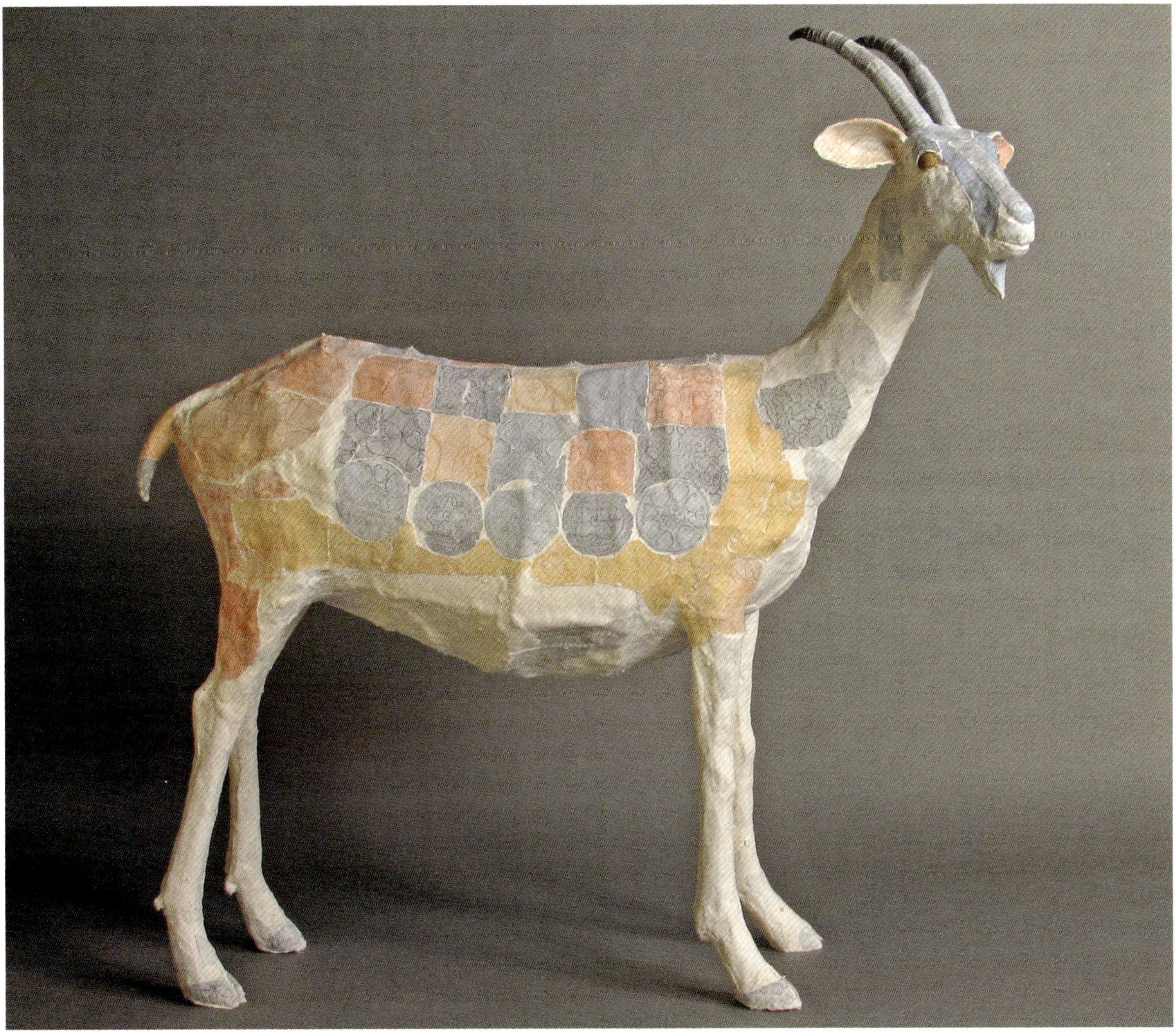

Sculpting and handbuilding

O'Byrne has devised a method for supporting the structure as she builds and fires. Nichrome wire is used to construct the torso armature of each animal, minus the legs. The individual wires are then covered with rods of paper to allow for shrinkage during drying and firing. Some wires, on the back of the animal, also have loops attached which will extend through the clay wall and allow the animal to be hung in the kiln, preventing slumping at top temperature. The armature is attached to wooden supports and tubes of paperclay are added to form legs. Fine sheets of paperclay are cast from slip on a plaster bat and applied to the armature. Once the entire animal has been covered, a second layer of porcelain paperclay is cast and applied over the first. Most of the modelling of features is completed at this stage. Hooves, tails and eyes are added. Approximately ten large sheets of patterned paperclay are created to form the final surface of the animal. The patterns are made by printing, drawing and scratching into coloured slips on a plaster bat. These pieces of pattered paperclay are then collaged onto the surface of the animal.

All animals are propped in the kiln and hung from the wire loops attached to the armature. The work is fired in a gas kiln to 1260°C (2300°F).

There is no reason to feel limited by the size of your kiln. Some especially large works can be built and fired in sections. Viola Frey perfected this technique, building her sizeable figures in several parts, and then constructing them post-firing.

Some artists carve or sculpt from a solid block of clay and then hollow out their sculptures and rejoin the pieces. Bonnie Smith uses this process, illustrated here.

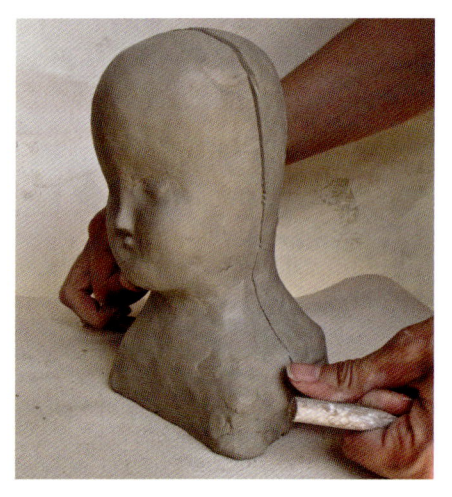

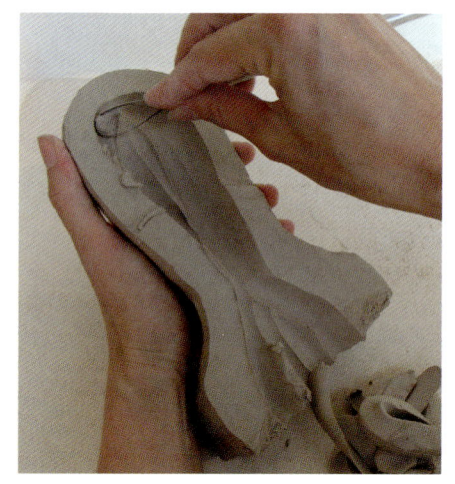

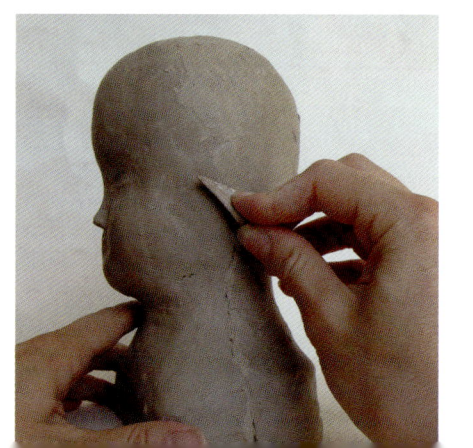

LEFT TO RIGHT FROM TOP:
Bonnie Smith, hollowing out a form. Step one is cutting the form in half.

Hollowing out a form with a loop tool.

Adding slip to the cross-hatched edges.

Sealing the join after reuniting the two halves.
Photos: Richard Holloway.

Handbuilding techniques

ABOVE, LEFT TO RIGHT: Jo Taylor hand-forming the elements of her sculpture, starting by creating a rough coil.

Applying the rough coil onto the bisque former.

Taylor's gestural motifs in the wet clay.
Photos: Andy Rose.

Bath-based ceramicist **Jo Taylor** makes sculptural forms from fragments of clay. Each fragment is created by a gesture of her hand. When the clay is very soft, it is formed into a rough coil and smeared onto a bisque surface, joining additional coils to form a basic motif. Each motif is different, and made quickly and instinctively. Using wet fingers, Taylor firmly brushes the clay until it takes the shape and direction of her gesture. Many pieces are made using this process. Each is left to dry a little before being removed and stored, and then assembled by scoring and joining.

For the artist, the experience of making is distinctly sensory. 'The making process is rhythmical and pleasurable, the sensation of the soft clay yielding. The finished sculptures contain a sense of energy and organic growth. The softness of the clay during the forming process remains apparent in the finished form, the fluid motion of the clay at the moment of its creation captured and contained in the final rigid structure.'

Taylor uses grogged clay. Its malleability is ideal for this free-form process and its strength enables her to produce large-scale work.

Working with clay

Working with ceramic materials can be confusing given the choice of clays, the possibilities of firing, and the range of work that can be made. Here are some tips and guidance to get you started.

Sculpting and handbuilding

Succession by Jo Taylor, 2012. Stoneware, height: 53 cm (21 in). *Photo: Andy Rose.*

Choosing clay

It's very easy to get tied up with which clay does what, and the array of clays can be overwhelming for a beginner. The traditional categories of earthenware, stoneware and porcelain are usually determined by firing temperature and the quality of the clay post-firing. These definitions are becoming somewhat blurred, with artists firing clays outside of their ranges, mixing opposing clays in one piece, and in some cases not firing the clay at all. As a guide, the maturing range for earthenware is usually around 1000–1180°C (1832–2156°F), for stoneware 1200–1300°C (2192–2372°F), and for porcelain 1240–1350°C (2264–2462°F).

Just as firing ranges can be imprecise, clays that are designed for particular uses, such as handbuilding or throwing, can be used for other purposes.

As a general rule, clays for handbuilding tend to be open, containing grog or other additives that reduce shrinkage rates and add strength. T-material is clay that fires to white or off-white, so is an ideal canvas for working with coloured slips or glazes. It is also plastic to work with and has a low shrinkage rate. Paperclay is also ideal for handbuilding. There are many resources on using paperclay or fibrous clay that are worth investigating, especially as this clay has specific qualities, one being that it can be fixed if cracks occur in the dry body. Clay for raku needs to withstand rapid heating and cooling so must be high in grog content to give an open, course body.

Small samples of clay are available from most suppliers, so it is a good idea to test some different clays, to get an idea of which is most suited to your project.

Drying and wrapping

Getting to grips with drying times is an essential skill when working with clay. You will learn a lot through trial and error, and much will depend on your particular working environment and methods – how wet is the clay as you begin the building process? How warm is your studio? How much are you handling and manipulating the clay? How large is the piece you are making? Are you building piece by piece or carving from a solid block? How complex are your joins? What other stresses might the clay be under?

All clay is subject to shrinkage to varying degrees. Shrinkage occurs throughout the drying and firing process – when the clay dries to bone dry, when it is bisque-fired and when it is fired to its highest temperature. Wrapping work thoroughly and allowing it to dry slowly can usually prevent cracks occurring due to shrinkage. Adding grog or sand to 'open' the clay texture also helps reduce shrinkage rates, but this does affect the clay's plasticity. You can test the shrinkage rates by rolling out a rectangular slab of clay 15 cm (6 in) in length, 4 cm (1½ in) in width, marking a 10 cm (4 in) line down the centre of the slab, and measuring the line at each stage of drying and firing.

If you are working on a piece in stages, wrap it well between working sessions. One thorough method is to wrap your form in damp newspaper and then wrap it in plastic. It is better to err on the side of caution, especially if you are just beginning to learn about the behaviour of clay in your particular working environment.

Cracks and breakages that occur in the kiln are often the result of the stress exerted on the clay during the drying process, especially in sculptural objects that are more inclined to be of varying thicknesses. If you are slow-drying a piece, be sure to check it as it dries in case hairline cracks appear – in the early stages of drying you can still mend these cracks.

If you are working with very wet clay and need to speed up the drying process, you can firm up the clay by using a hairdryer or gas torch. Keep the hairdryer or torch moving around the form as you dry. Don't stay in one spot too long, don't force-dry any joins or stress points this way, and only dry to firm the work up a little bit so it can support itself, rather than trying to dry until the clay is leatherhard.

Firing and kilns

Firing can be a daunting prospect for the uninitiated, but there are many resources and manufacturers' guidelines to help you. In most cases ceramicists and potters opt for electric kilns as they are straightforward, reliable, easily controlled and suit most studio spaces. There are various other types of kiln available and many ways of building your own kiln – there is an abundance of literature and video tutorials to guide you.

Before purchasing a kiln, consider your electricity or fuel supply, the type of work you will be making, the physical demands of packing a kiln and where it will be sited.

Firing your kiln economically and packing it efficiently can be difficult with handbuilt objects that are irregular in shape, so taking some time to plan the packing is useful. Where possible, make the most of the firing by including small test pieces and test tiles to progress your research.

Pyrometric cones are used to measure the kiln temperature accurately. Cones are especially helpful if you are developing your surfaces with glaze materials. Clay and glaze results depend on the temperature reached and the time exposed to heat – the cones measure both these things. Place them inside the kiln in line with the spy-hole, so you can watch them bending as the kiln reaches temperature. Always wear goggles when observing this and open the spy-holes wearing heavy-duty gloves.

Finally, if you are in the development stages, be fastidious about recording your firing results. Keep a note of the materials applied, your firing cycles, the melting point of the cones and then analyse the work once it is fired.

If you are experimenting with colours, clays or structures that could run, crack or break during firing then it is worth firing in a saggar to protect your kiln. Saggars are usually constructed of coarse clay and can be all shapes and sizes depending on what you are using them for; they can be open or lidded.

Firing cycles

For simple round structures such as pots and thin-walled pieces increasing the kiln temperature evenly up to your required temperature then allowing the kiln to cool naturally is usual studio practice. If your work becomes larger and more complex you may need to adapt the way it is fired, for instance firing slowly so as to minimize the pressure on the piece.

Although there are no strict firing rules, it's important to understand the various changes that occur, especially before and around 600°C (1112°F). Even a dry piece of work has water in the clay molecules. During firing, as the kiln temperature increases steam is formed and pressure builds up in the piece. If the water can't escape quickly enough, cracks will appear or explosions will occur, firing slowly allows time for slow and consistent evaporation. The firing can then be speeded up after 600°C to the top temperature.

How slowly you fire at the start will depend on the nature of your work – simple constructions and thinly built pieces may require 100°C (212°F) per hour up to 600°C, whereas a complex carved, multi layered structure may only survive if you fire at 40°C (104°F) per hour up to 600°C. Trial and error is part of the firing and it can be a frustrating process to learn. Many problems can be addressed by thorough drying of work, especially carved or complex pieces, and by firing slowly.

Other information on the firing process can be found at www.pottery.about.com and www.ceramicartsdaily.org. The European Ceramic Work Centre book, *The Ceramic Process*, (A&C Black, 2005) gives a comprehensive explanation of the firing process, along with sample firing cycles.

A small saggar, used to protect the kiln from unstable substances.
Photo: John Taylor.

Health and safety

Clay dust is a perpetual problem. It contains silica, which is harmful if inhaled over a period of time. Dust is hard to get rid of entirely, but you can manage it by routinely wetting down and wiping surfaces with a damp sponge. Never brush or dust floors, as this releases the particles into the air – instead, mop or vacuum, or do both. Clean your tools, wash-cloths, aprons and towels regularly. Ventilate your space and work with open windows where possible.

Keep storage areas and equipment clear of dust, too. Wipe down shelves, workbenches, banding wheels and boards, and any other equipment that comes into contact with clay, wet or dry.

Observe the hazard warnings on all glaze and other materials, which should be labelled and stored appropriately, away from children and pets. Always wear a respirator mask and surgical gloves when mixing powdered glazes, and wear surgical gloves to handle glaze in its wet state, too. Cover any cuts or wounds to prevent contamination by ceramic materials. Keep a first-aid box in your studio and ensure it is always well stocked.

Food and drink should not be consumed in the studio. Kitchen and glaze utensils should always be kept apart.

Notes
[1] Antony Quinn, Introduction, *Firing Up Handbook*, Crafts Council, London, 2010.
[2] Betty Blandino, *Coiled Pottery: Traditional and Contemporary Ways*, A&C Black, London, 1984.

Eliza Day.

2 Research and inspiration

'The things I discover in the act of drawing inspire how I will sculpt the piece in clay.'[1] Cynthia Lahti

Working with ceramics is a juggling act. Form, function, surface, concept, scale, technique and material all play a part to varying degrees. Clay is an extremely versatile substance, but many processes are time-consuming, and glazing and firing use up valuable resources, so it is often useful and necessary to do your thinking and planning in other, quicker mediums. Similarly, when faced with so many possibilities for inspiration, finding your focus can be tricky. This chapter looks at various approaches to research and development, and the different ways that artists generate ideas.

Be wary of the one-size-fits-all approach; instead, try to find the mix of methods that work for you. Sculptor David Hicks says, 'For me building and thinking physically is the only way to work out ideas. My ideas are meant to exist in three dimensions.'[2] Working in sketchbooks is not for everybody. There are many different possibilities if you are looking for a place to start and you will always find that, by exploring a variety of methods, unexpected things will be discovered.

Look around you

Your immediate environment is an extremely fertile location for inspiration and there are lots of ways to experiment with your surroundings and generate ideas for a ceramic response. Observe the objects you use every day – the prints and patterns around you, the voices and noises you encounter. Sketch the screen as you watch TV, draw the imagined faces of radio presenters, or make marks with the earth from a garden. Try drawing the view from your window onto your window (or onto an attached acetate sheet) in marker pen. Model in response to a favourite possession with air-drying clay or dug-up earth. For new forms, look at the shapes that shadows throw, or explore an object out of sight with one hand, while drawing what you feel with the other. There are many other creative drawing exercises and resources for you to experiment with.

Your local museum or art gallery, church, shopping centre, pub or park will often present ideas and source material. It is also useful to research artists who inspire you and examine what goes into their work. Another approach is to plunder your personal life. If there are interests, hobbies or particular beliefs that fascinate you, look to these for a place to begin.

LEFT: Stephen Bird, *Drawing for Eliza Day 3*, 2011. Ink on paper, 28 x 20 cm (11 x 8 in). Photo: Artist and Rex Irwin, Art Dealer.

Sculpting and handbuilding

Makiko Hastings in her studio with a wall of images including drawings, patterns, photos.
Photo: Makiko Hastings.

Construct a working environment that inspires you. You may benefit from calm, white walls with just the view from your studio window, or the sounds of the street. Assembling a wall of images – collected photos, postcards, previous pieces, artists who inspire, found objects, organic matter, artworks or indeed anything you find visually exciting – can help you to develop your aesthetic and generate ideas.

Claire Loder's studio wall and work bench, with collected objects, magazine images, photos and sketches.
Photo: John Taylor.

Research and inspiration

Fenella Elms' test pieces on her workshop windowsill.
Photo: David Parmiter.

Emma Rodgers working in her studio with her pet hare.
Photo: Jay Goldmark.

49

Sculpting and handbuilding

Sketches in clay: models used by Lilly Zuckerman as sketches to generate ideas. *Photo: Lilly Zuckerman.*

Models and maquettes

For some artists, the intuitive nature of their process is hindered by too much planning. They prefer to dive straight in. For others, working out their ideas in three dimensions at the start, in the form of small models, is the best method. A model formed in the hand, roughly-sculpted, can give a sense of the composition of the piece, and its scale and structure.

Lilly Zuckerman uses 'clay sketches' to develop new forms: 'When I'm out of ideas I will give myself 20lbs of clay in 1lb balls and spend 1–2 minutes on each. The speed and lack of preciousness allows me to test ideas quickly. Then I'll go back and test smaller ideas on the forms – cut a wall down, fold this, cut it in half, etc. If I get three ideas out of the exercise it was worth it. I have many of these scattered around my table. If I can't achieve the idea or just want to hang onto it, I'll fire the little model. They are very rough but hold enough of an idea. Those are my sketchbook.'

Jenny Southam uses small, fast, three-dimensional models or maquettes of pieces that she intends to make to help her resolve problems within a current piece, in terms of the relative sizes of components and their structure, form and balance. 'They often end up being very intimate pieces, imbued with an emotional vitality that can be difficult to reproduce in a larger version!'

Research and inspiration

Drawing and painting

For some ceramicists, drawing and painting play a significant part in their practice. Some produce bodies of work quite separate from their clay work. Others work in sketchbooks or notebooks, developing the form, subject and surface simultaneously.

There is an interesting parity evident in the work of some ceramicists – it is easy to see the symbiosis between the drawing and ceramic work. **Elke Sada**'s drawings are one such example. Examining her drawings, it would be easy to conclude that they 'translate' well 'into' ceramics. Sada is drawing whether she has a brush loaded with ink or one loaded with slip. Her work is intuitive, expressive and exudes energy, on paper or clay. There is a planning function to her drawings on paper: they help to explore colour and surface, and it's a quick way to generate and capture ideas for ceramic vessels, but she shows the same confidence, mastery of materials and delight in the process in any medium. For her, though, there are some important distinctions

Elke Sada, *Black Cloud*, drawing, 2007. *Photo: courtesy of the artist.*

Sculpting and handbuilding

Stephanie Quayle, drawing of a fox. *Photo: courtesy of the artist.*

to make: 'The difference is that clay needs more patience for drying and the result changes a lot with the firing. Drawing doesn't need an equipped workshop and I enjoy that I can do it wherever, whenever.'

There is also a close relationship between the two-dimensional and three-dimensional to be found in the work of Jo Taylor.

Potter **Kyra Cane** discusses her love of landscape, what drawing it means to her, and the role it plays in her practice. 'Drawing is central to the way I think. It is the method by which I absorb information, it helps me to look and to remember. The thread that has run throughout my life is my love of landscape, and the aspect of this that is my current obsession is edges. It can simply be the dark edge of a cloud in relation to hedgerows, or the more spectacular relationship between that of land, sea and sky. Materials relate to circumstance as much as anything else and I often work in black and white before I use colour. I draw anywhere, but especially when I visit museums, as it helps me to prioritise. I am attracted to strong forms, loving objects that are also simple and straightforward.'

Cane's drawing practice runs parallel to her ceramic work, as she does not work directly from drawings. Her sketchbooks and drawings are private, forming 'a resource mainly through the process of their making'. Kyra also uses photography to capture the landscape, taking photos that make up series of gently distinct images.

Research and inspiration

Jo Taylor, *Drawing*, 2012. Acrylic on paper, 60 x 42 cm (23½ x 16½ in). *Photo: Andy Rose.*

Kyra Cane, *Pembrokeshire Coast IV*, 2005. Charcoal on paper, 58 x 75 cm (22¾ x 29½ in). *Photo: Mike Simmons.*

Sculpting and handbuilding

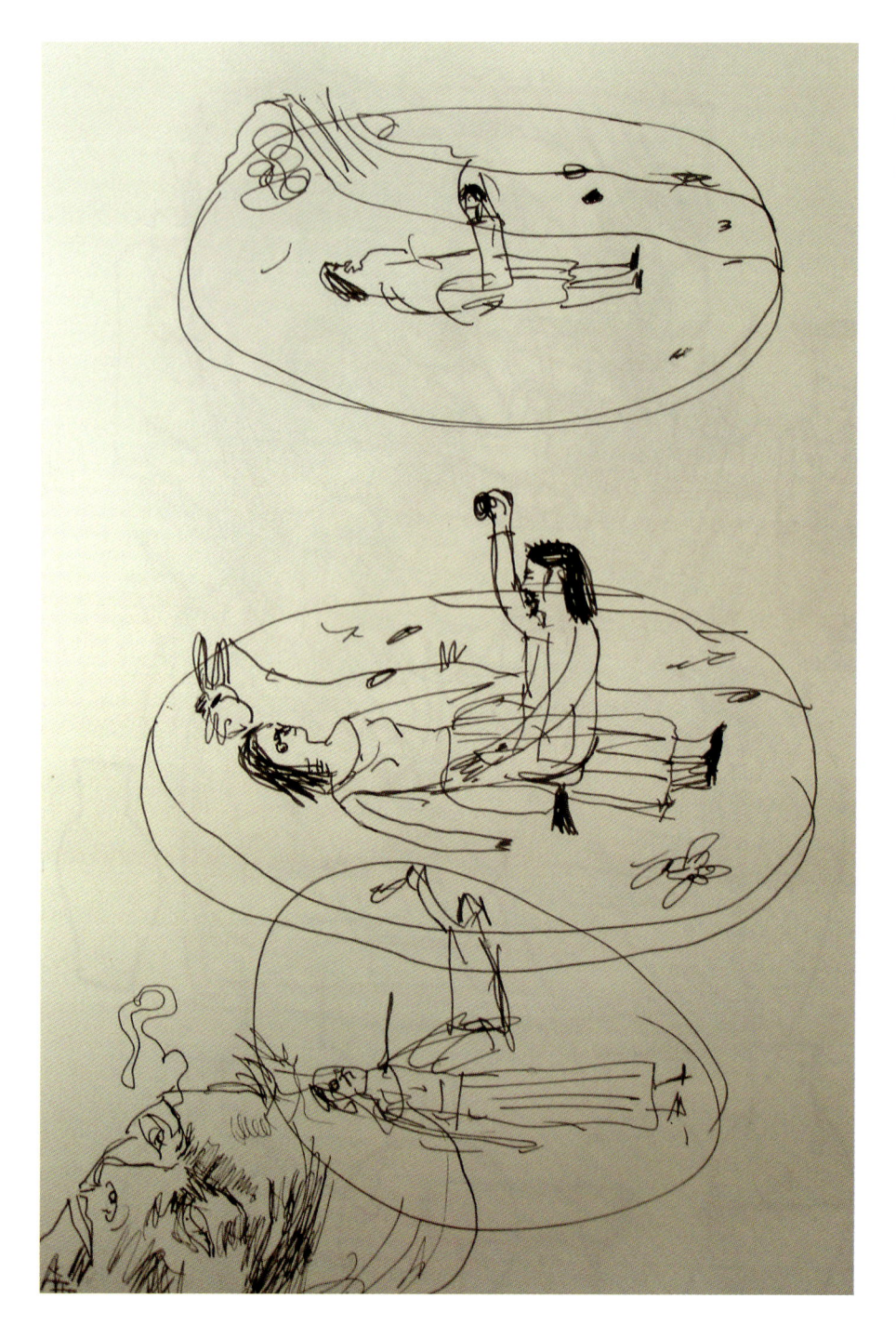

Stephen Bird, *Drawing for Eliza Day 2*, 2011. Ink on paper, 35 x 52 cm (13¾ x 20½ in). *Photo: Artist and Rex Irwin, art dealer.*

Stephen Bird's drawing production runs parallel to his ceramic work. The example here shows a relatively detailed and finished pen ink and wash drawing. This drawing acts as a reference point for a piece of ceramic work. From this, Stephen makes a series of quick sketches to help him plan the ceramic sculpture.

54

Research and inspiration

ABOVE: Stephen Bird, *Eliza Day*, 2011. Clay, pigment, glaze, 16 x 22 x 18 cm (6¼ x 8¾ x 7 in). *Photo: Artist and Rex Irwin, art dealer.*

RIGHT: Stephen Bird, *Drawing for Staffordshire Psycho*, 2011. Ink on paper, 32 x 20 x 16 cm (12½ x 8 x 6¼ in). *Photo: Artist and Rex Irwin, art dealer.*

55

Sculpting and handbuilding

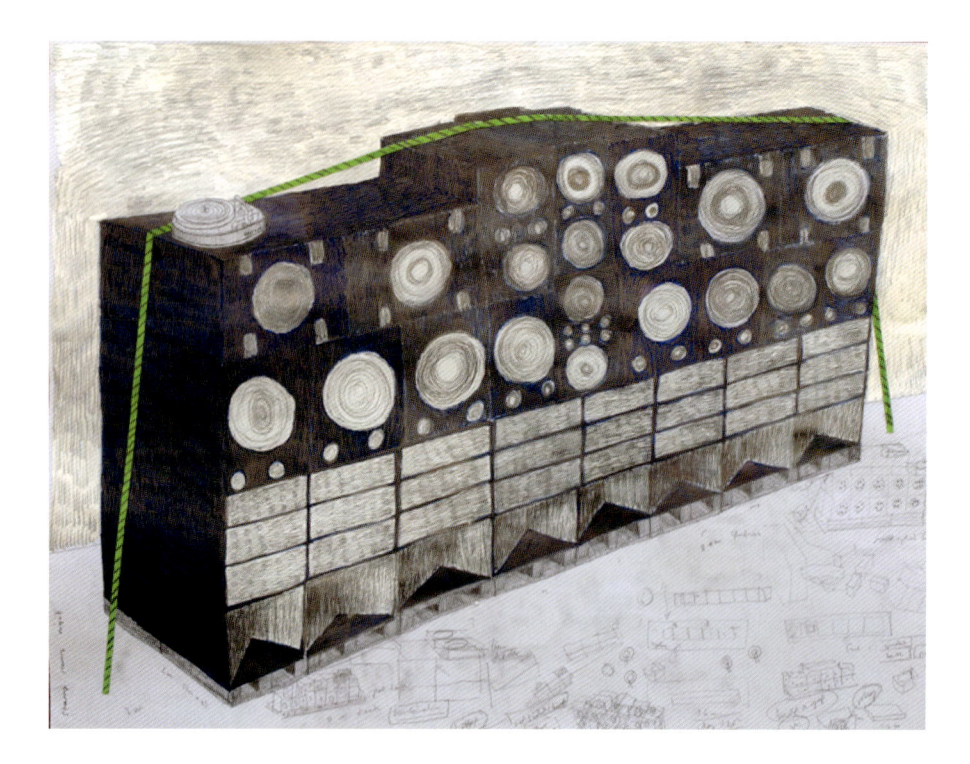

Keith Harrison, *Night Float*, 2011. Drawing for Jerwood Makers Open, pencil, felt tip, Tippex, 84 x 59 cm (33 x 23¼ in). *Photo: Keith Harrison.*

Jerwood Makers Open 2011 prize-winner **Keith Harrison** draws because 'on paper all things are possible'. Harrison makes performative work that is highly complex and relies on detailed planning. Although some of his drawings are a schematic tool for such planning, the initial drawings are alive with his excitement for the project.

Drawing plays a significant role in Manuel Canu's practice. Using a range of materials and processes such as black ink, lino-cutting and dry point etching, Canu produces drawings that represent both real and imagined places. Using the same inspiration sources as his installations, the drawings focus on buildings, living rooms, vases and pieces of furniture. He produces ceramic works and drawings in parallel, as they complement each other. In some cases, the drawings work as a map for the making of future installations, and vice versa: some installations are later turned into drawings. Canu also takes inspiration from the stories he hears about the buildings he is working in.

Swedish artist **Maria Kristofersson** produces gently asymmetric forms using earthenware clay. A fascination with 'whitenesses' means Kristofersson continually experiments with different clays and finishes. The majority of her pieces are coil-built. With an expressive rather than a controlled approach, Kristofersson achieves her trademark naïve, informal shapes. Sitting somewhere between utility and art object, her vessels stem from a strong interest in drawing and painting; the bold yet wavering lines, a recurring motif throughout her work, are evidence of this. Her life drawings are confident and animated. The angular way in which she renders the line on paper to describe a figure is abstracted, and translated with efficiency and energy onto the clay.

FACING PAGE, TOP LEFT: Manuel Canu, *Vase and Pattern 1*, 2011. Black ink and paper, 70 x 50 cm (27½ x 19¾ in). *Photo: Ole Akhøj.*

TOP RIGHT: Maria Kristofersson, drawing, 2005, Pencil, papertape, 29 x 21 cm (11½ x 8¼ in). *Photo: Maria Kristofersson.*

BOTTOM: Maria Kristofersson, *Object*, 2010. Earthenware, glaze, 6 x 30 x 20 cm (2½ x 11¾ x 8 in). *Photo: Maria Kristofersson.*

Research and inspiration

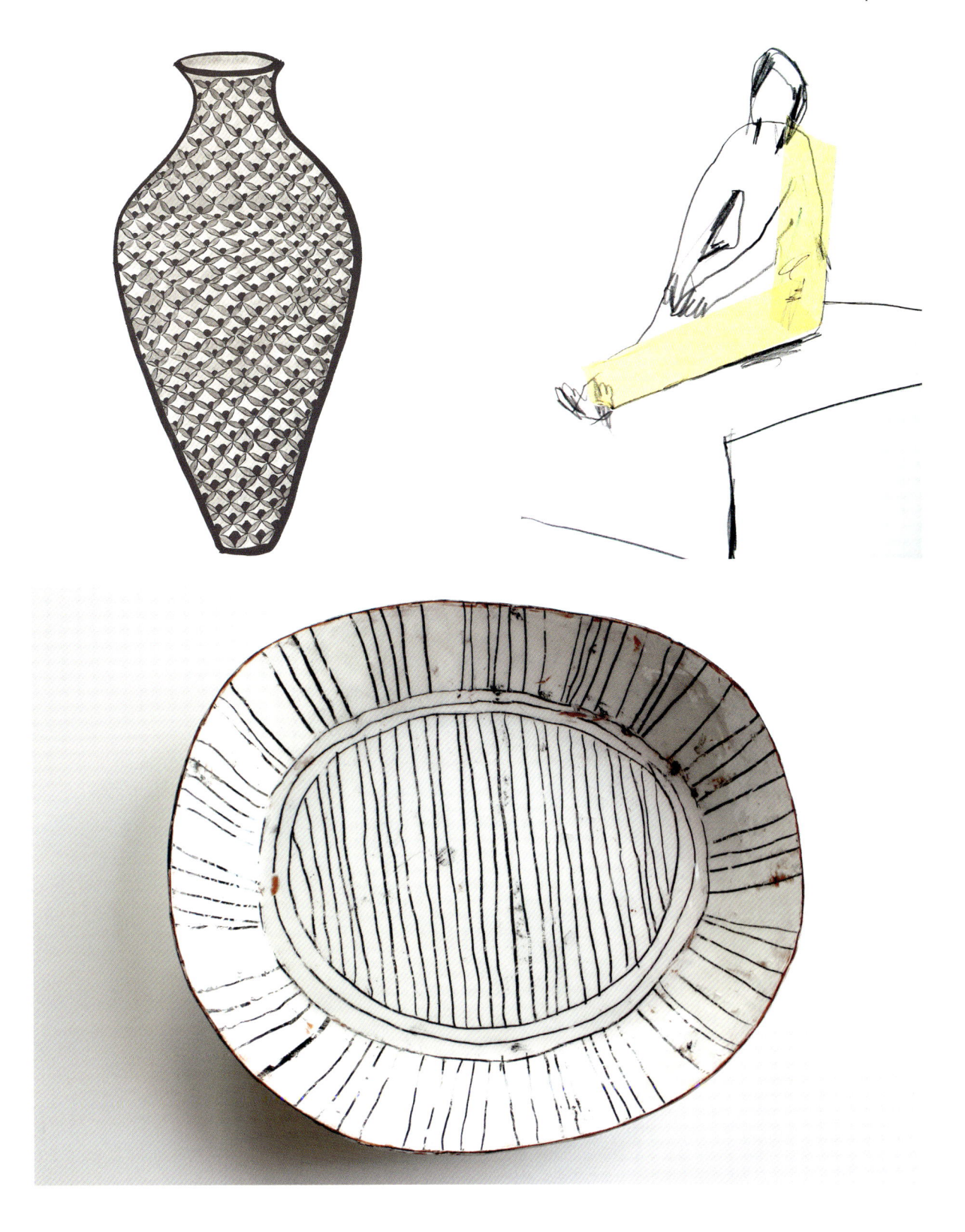

Sculpting and handbuilding

Sketchbooks

No two sketchbooks are the same – they are as varied as the people who use them and can serve many functions. They can be a place for quick sketches, note taking, to gather together the artists you admire, or reference images. Whether highly portable or tome-like, they are what you make them.

For **Jenny Southam**, her sketchbooks have two distinct roles. One type of sketchbook contains her development and planning sketches and ideas for particular ceramic sculptures. The other type, purely for drawing, is by no means isolated from her ceramic work – in fact, they play a significant role: 'I feel that these are a vital part of my artistic activity; they keep my drawing fluid, they encourage me to maintain a continuous process of engaging with the landscape and with my environment, wherever I happen to be, and they serve to keep me noticing and cataloguing details, colours, shapes, forms and textures.'

Makiko Hastings lives and works in North Yorkshire. A recent graduate of Harrogate College, Hastings works with stoneware and porcelain, throwing and handbuilding mainly functional objects. She is strongly influenced by the importance of the food culture and family table gatherings of her native Japan. Another important aspect of her work is drawing, and specifically the idea of 'rakugaki', meaning doodling. Hastings says she 'draws whatever comes into her mind'. An avid photographer, blogger and collector of things, she surrounds herself with images, patterns and found objects, building a library of references that augments her distinctive visual language. She is interested in the equivalence of ceramic and non-ceramic materials and is continually looking for ways to 'translate' the line drawings she develops in her sketchbooks onto or into her ceramic objects.

Jenny Southam's sketchbooks. *Photo: John Melville.*

Research and inspiration

Makiko Hastings' sketchbook page.
Photo: Makiko Hastings.

BELOW: Watercolour sketches by Claire Loder.
Photo: Claire Loder.

Digital tools

Various software can be helpful in designing your handbuilt work, especially in developing the surface treatment if you are working with drawn elements that will become decals. **Lucy Foakes'** canopic jars start with an intensive research period focusing on her subject. She reads biographies, watches documentaries, films, videos and interviews, and explores the wider subjects of fame, death and anatomy; this research results in the hand-drawn decals that adorn her jars. The original drawings are scanned and Foakes uses Photoshop to add colour. For the focal point of each piece, the jar lid, which is either laser-cut acrylic or water-jet-cut metal, Foakes creates the design using Adobe Illustrator or CAD software. (See more on Foakes on p. 72.)

Sculpting and handbuilding

Lucy Foakes' sketches for *Elvis* and *Frida Kahlo* canopic jars, 2009. *Photo: Lucy Foakes.*

Online inspiration

The Internet is packed with interesting sights and sounds; almost every real-world site or activity has its online counterpart. It's an incredibly abundant, if somewhat overwhelming, place for research.

Visual artists have been quick to populate the Internet, making use of sites such as Facebook, Twitter, Pinterest, Instagram, Tumblr, YouTube, Vimeo, Blogger, Etsy and Folksy along with various portfolio sites, so you can find out about their work and get a unique insight into their practices. The opportunities for exchanging skills, networking in an international arena, exploring new markets unfettered by real-world limitations and making connections with other artists at various stages of their careers and in all corners of the globe are manifold. Many sites overlap in their functions and artists tend to use a combination to reach different audiences. The Internet is quick to adapt and adopt. Like anything else, it is about finding out what works for you, whether for research purposes or if you chose to develop an online presence – although the beauty of the Internet is that these two functions are intertwined.

Research and inspiration

Cynthia Lahti, *Black Cat*, 2008. Ink on tissue paper. A drawing of an image Lahti found in a French magazine. It is a large, aggressive rendering using ink on archival tissue paper. The tissue paper has a fragile quality to it that, for Lahti, evokes preciousness.

Photography

Photography has often played a significant role in artists' practice. Some use it to create work, others use it to collect or generate source material or as a process to help think through their ideas. Apart from recording your ceramic work as you make it, it can be useful to experiment with photography to see what ideas it throws up. Try photographing your work in different contexts, settings and groupings, or taking close-up shots of your surfaces.

Notes
[1] Cynthia Lahti, artist's statement.
[2] David Hicks, artist's statement.

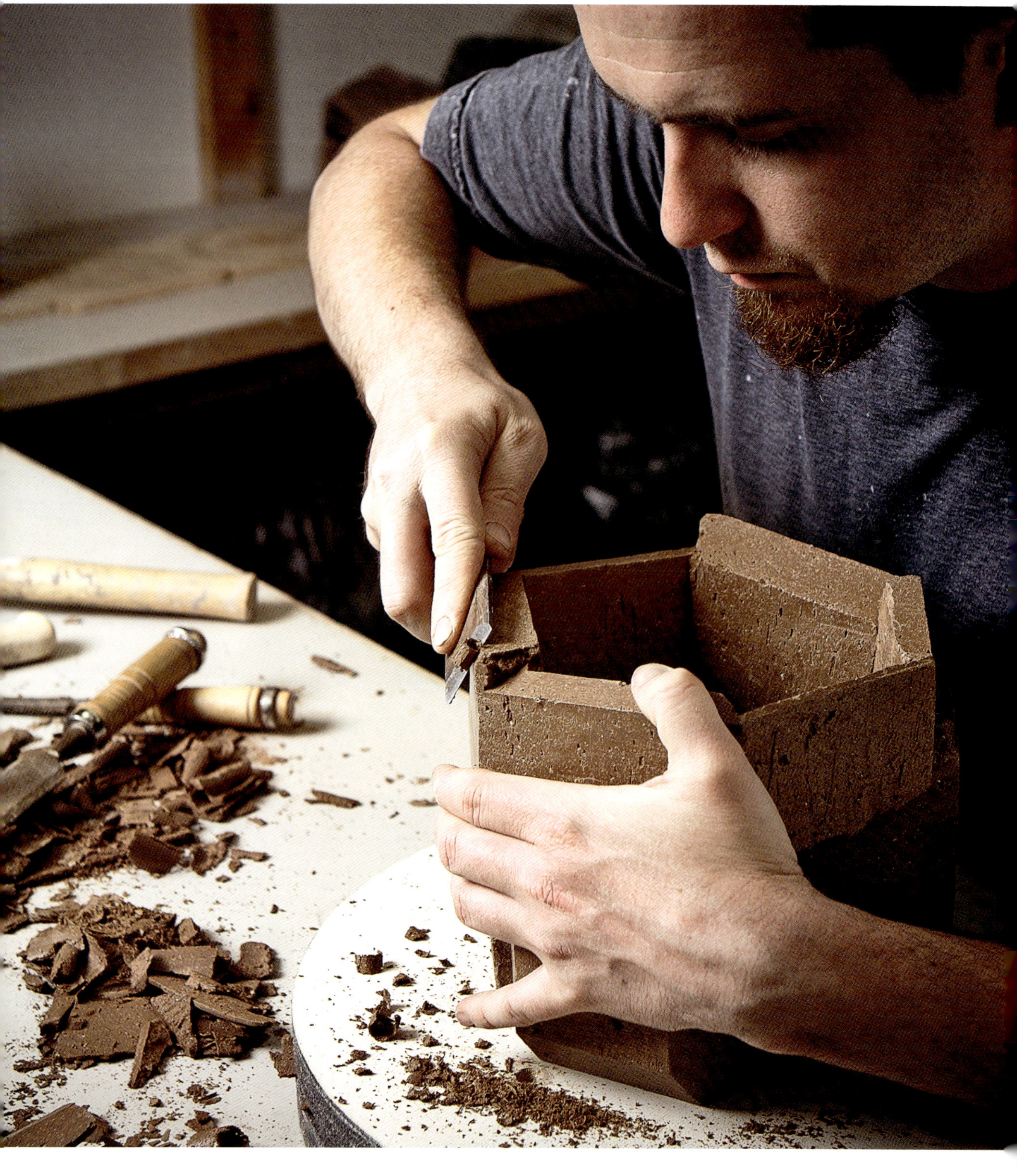

3 The vessel

'The vessel is persistent and keeps being made down through the ages, mute and compliant, but articulate in the way that it reflects us back to ourselves.'[1]
Natasha Daintry

The history of humankind is bound up with the history of clay and utility. Ceramic objects have a long tradition of being used, held and touched, none more so than the vessel. The field of ceramics has travelled far from its pottery roots and is much changed since the anodyne image of the 'brown pot', which seemed to embody popular perception of mid-20th century production. But it is still difficult to disentangle contemporary ceramic practice from its historic terminology of pots, pottery and crockery. Some artists would welcome a clean break, while for others the history of the ceramic vessel is a fertile hunting ground.

With the emergence of non-functional vessels, clay has been commandeered to express the notional and abstract. These art objects are sometimes aloof – less easily experienced directly by the hands, designed to be admired from afar or exhibited in galleries where touch is discouraged. Despite this, the material of clay makes the association of utility and touch unbreakable. The tactile magnetism remains, which keeps function and the vessel uppermost in our hands and minds. In *The Pot Book*, Edmund De Waal calls the vessel 'inexhaustible'.[2] This age-old template of ceramic output always was and continues to be a thriving area of investigation for ceramic artists.

The simplest handbuilt vessel is a pinch pot, formed from a ball of clay in a cupped palm, but handbuilt vessels can be many things. This chapter explores a variety of vessels and offers some starting points.

We often tend to think of functional vessels being thrown on the wheel, a hangover from the days of factory production. Handbuilt forms can mimic wheel-thrown or cast items; you can build the form with precision, and finesse the surface to reproduce the uniformity of these other processes. Although throwing can be an incredibly fast way to produce pots, handbuilding techniques offer greater creative freedom. Hand-formed objects can tell the story of the maker. Many ceramicists and potters elect to use handbuilding techniques to produce functional ware precisely because the outcome is not regular, symmetric or standardised. There is a poetic beauty to the cup that bears the fingertip indentations of the maker, or a bowl that reveals its coiled construction in unsmoothed walls. A piece formed in the cupped hands of the maker can fit the user's cupped hands beautifully, providing a tactile experience as well as an aesthetic and practical one.

LEFT: Jonathan Cross at work carving a vessel form.
Photo: Darren Looker.

Sculpting and handbuilding

Stephen Bird, *Man stick and dog shit*, 2011. Tin-glazed earthenware plate, 33 x 44 cm (13 x 17¼ in). *Photo: Artist and Rex Irwin, art dealer.*

Functional and non-functional

Making utility ware can mean that you are bound by certain ergonomic conventions. You may want to consider these and let them guide you or entirely reject them. But there are certain practicalities you cannot overlook: a glaze that comes into contact with food needs to be lead-free or non-toxic (if buying glazes look for the 'recommended for tableware pictograph or ask your supplier) and if you are making a cup to hold boiling liquid, the handle needs to stay on! The object needs to feel comfortable in the hand and good to the touch – not necessarily smooth and soft, but an engaging tactile experience. An everyday item needs to be simple to clean and cups must be easy to drink from. Consider the weight of a cup once boiling water is added. Also, how does the cup balance when full? How much heat is transmitted from the body of the cup to the fingers that hold the handle? Avoid overtly scratchy textures, rough edges or sharp handles. Working with a banding wheel helps when building vessels as they are usually built to be experienced 'in the round'. The banding wheel allows you to view and rotate the pieces as you work. If your vessel is functional you will need to consider how it sits on the surface. The bottom edge will need to withstand repeated contact with a hard surface. Consider adding a foot ring or bevelling the bottom edge.

Elke Sada constructing a
slab form, painted with slips.
Photo: Dennis Conrad.

Making effective and beautiful functional ware is a very particular area of ceramics. As soon as you start tinkering with the lore of the everyday object, your vessels enter new territory and you are somewhat freer to roam.

The early 20th century saw artists such as Picasso and Chagall experiment with ceramics, bringing their distinct voices and fine art aesthetics to functional and sculptural clay objects. In the post-war years in the UK, the dominance of thrown ware was challenged by a unique combination of things. New ways of teaching in various art schools encouraged a generation of potters to explore fresh territories; the work of émigrés Lucie Rie and Hans Coper had a significant influence and provided a counter to the strict functionality of Leach; and the contemporary art movement of the 1960s blurred the lines between material and function and sculpture and pottery, heralding a universal 'freeing-up' across the art and craft world.

Which technique suits which vessel?

A vessel can be built using any of the methods outlined in Chapter 1. Some techniques lend themselves to particular types of vessel, but each offers many possibilities, and it is worth exploring what the different processes can achieve.

Sculpting and handbuilding

Sarah Purvey, *Landscape Series Drift*, 2012. Coil-built, Valentine Black Clay, slips, unglazed. Fired to 1160°C (2120°F) in an electric kiln, 44 x 49 x 35 cm (17¼ x 19¼ x 13¾ in). *Photo: John Taylor.*

Coiled vessels

Traditionally, voluminous jugs and big-bellied pots were built using the coiling technique. Coiling played a significant role in Africa; pottery traditions developed without the potter's wheel, so handbuilding was the primary process. The early potters sat on the ground, resting their pot in front of them on a disc or mat, using their legs to balance the structure and rotating it as they built.

Coiling is ideal for curved organic forms. The coils can be manipulated to attain the form you require by pulling up or out, and by varying the thickness. Coiled vessels can also be built quickly. Varying the type of coil will have an influence on the vessel's form and function; flat, ribbon coils can result in a softly faceted surface, while a functional coiled object with fat coils will be heavy when liquid or food is added, but will conduct less heat. This type of vessel will take longer to heat up but will retain its heat.

Using a banding wheel as you coil will allow you to easily rotate and view your vessel. If you are constructing a particularly large piece consider building the vessel upside-down – this will help support the weight of the clay as you build. Start with the largest coil first, for the mouth of the pot, then gradually reduce the size of the coils as you build towards the base.

Makiko Hastings, *Mazekoze*, rectangular plate detail, 2012. Sgraffito, 24 x 12 cm (9½ x 4¾ in). *Photo: Makiko Hastings.*

Slab-built vessels

Historically, vessels such as dishes, boxes and plates have been produced by slab-building with clay, the flat surface offering the best canvas for decoration. An angular or geometric vessel is most easily built using leatherhard slabs. Slabs in this state allow for precise cut lines, helping you to assemble the vessel with accuracy. If your vessel is large, it will need to be built from clay that has the strength to support itself.

Slabs can also be used for more fluid forms. Moulded round a former, such as a cardboard tube or kiln prop, a slab can easily take on the shape of a container. Simple mugs can be made in this way, finished off with the addition of a slab, coil-built handle or pulled handle. A heavily-grogged clay will not bend or curve as well as a finer clay. The dryness of the clay is important, especially with functional vessels, where cracks aren't desirable. The clay needs to be soft enough to join well, but stiff enough to maintain its shape.

Pinched and sculpted

Pinching is a beginner's technique but it is also a method that offers great creative potential. Pinching overlaps with sculpting; fingertip manipulation and response to the clay is common to both techniques. A pinch pot is the simplest vessel and pinching was probably the earliest clay technique. From a pinch pot base, you can form a basic cup or build an intricate, complex vessel. With fingers or tools, the surface can be modelled, or the pinch marks left intact.

Ingrid Bathe makes delicate, pinched porcelain forms that exhibit a clear trace of the maker and communicate a thoughtful approach and calm intention (see p. 68). 'I want the process of creation to be visible to the viewer,' she says. 'When two pieces of clay are joined together I leave a seam line; each pinched mark is left intact so when looked at closely my fingerprints can be seen.'

Sculpting and handbuilding

Ingrid Bathe, *Oval platter with handles*, 2011. Porcelain paperclay, 8 x 28 x 18 cm (3 x 11 x 7 in). *Photo: courtesy of the artist.*

Bathe mixes the clay from dry materials and adds paper fibre to increase the green strength. After pinching the clay to achieve the desired form, a thin layer of glaze is applied on the inside. The outside remains unglazed. Fired, the glaze has a blue or purple tone depending on which light it is being viewed under, daylight or fluorescent. The clay is fired to a high temperature, cone 10. It is vitrified, translucent and begins to flux so that the unglazed portions of the piece have a slight sheen to them. Bathe fires in reduction, which gives the white porcelain clay a cool, bluish tint.

Carving

Starting with a solid block enables you to carve deep into the surface. The weight of the clay lends itself more to a sculpted vessel than a functional one, although a fine clay, intricately-carved and small-scale, can still serve as a functional object.

Starting points

There are many superb reference books if you want to explore vessels further. Local and national museums hold collections, and you can visit potteries, galleries and exhibitions. Or just look around you – each of us is surrounded by manufactured or natural objects that hold, gather, encase, surround or envelop. If research doesn't appeal and you want to learn by getting stuck in, take Lilly Zuckerman's example of making clay 'sketches' (p. 50).

It is precisely because the vessel is so commonplace that it makes a great starting point for anybody experimenting with clay. Making a simple vessel, working with a concept so recognisable, allows you to set aside any worries about planning and is a perfect approach for the less experienced. Just sink your thumb into a ball of clay and see where it takes you.

Beirut-born **Nathalie Khayat** builds vessel forms, finding inspiration in the 'infinitely small, the almost invisible'. Intrigued by the seed as the 'prime vessel', her starting point is the photographic enlargement of grains from microscopic flowers. The resulting

Frankie Locke, *Curved Form*, 2009. Carved stoneware, 13 x 17 x 13 cm (5 x 6¾ x 5 in). *Photo: John Taylor.*

Nathalie Khayat, *Seed 2*, 2011. Texture printed in porcelain slabs, unglazed, 30 x 45 cm (11¾ x 17¾ in). *Photo: Elie Bekhazi.*

organic structures are far from negligible: they are fluid, robust and decorative, without being frivolous or visually distracting. Her sculptures are expressive and informal, and although there is an ordered repetitiveness in some of her textured surfaces, the forms themselves are unordered and asymmetric – a nod to the unruly chaos of nature. Some pieces are large in scale, like her *Premature Blossoms*, and all bear the mark of Khayat's hands. 'I rarely use tools,' Khayat says. 'The majority of time, I let my fingers do the work by pushing the clay in or out to create indentations or bumps.'

Nathalie Khayat, *Seed 2*, 2011. Texture printed in porcelain slabs, unglazed, 30 x 45 cm (11¾ x 17¾ in). *Photo: Elie Bekhazi.*

She builds the structure first then adds the layers that define the form. 'Through that work, I explore themes that are of interest to me: sound, rhythm and vibration, inner silence and landscape, stillness and movement.' Khayat uses porcelain for its whiteness, purity and translucent qualities – she often leaves it unglazed. Other pieces are built in stoneware, glazed and raku-fired.

Amy Jane Hughes' *Trésor Découvert* (*Treasure Uncovered*) series is a conversation with a very specific point in ceramic history. Using various handbuilding methods (coiling, press-moulding and sprigging), Hughes re-imagines the tightly controlled *objets d'art* of the French Royal Sèvres Factory in the late 17th and 18th centuries. Hughes describes how these prestigious porcelain wares 'carried no visible suggestion of their material identity and [were] so lavishly decorated that each detail was left in competition on the surface, striving to attract attention.' By comparison with the original wares, Hughes' vessels are delightfully rough-hewn forms. They are irreverent, but maintain a referential decadence; while echoing the Sèvres wares, they celebrate the material qualities of the clay. The expressive nature of the making is evident. It allows us to imagine Hughes' hands on the clay as the vessels take form.

Lisa Stockham makes slab-built vessels from sections of clay imprinted with patterned texture. Some vessels are handbuilt from small, individual press-moulded sections or fragments. Strongly influenced by textile imagery, Stockham produces clay slabs that imitate sheets of fabric or frayed material. Focusing on a decorative detail, the motif is repeated and pushed to the extreme.

ABOVE: Amy Jane Hughes, *Trésor Découvert Series*, 2010. Handbuilt lidded vessels (coiled, press-moulded, sprigged) with gold lustre detailing. Each piece approx. 45 x 25 cm (17¾ x 9¾ in). *Photo: Ester Segarra.*

Lisa Stockham, *Fool's Gold*, 2009. Earthenware, bronze glaze, press-moulded squares, 40 x 25 cm (15¾ x 9¾ in). *Photo: Dominic Tschudin.*

Lucy Foakes, *Demeter's Prize*, 2011. Ceramic and acrylic, 50 x 30 cm (19¾ x 11¾ in). *Photo: Ash Buttle.*

She contrasts this repetition and order with a dissolving form. 'The objects I create often appear to be crumbling, breaking down to formlessness,' she says. 'It is as if the form has been rebuilt from remains, becoming reminiscent of eroding sculptures or mended crockery.'

Stockham combines slab-building with coiling and press-moulding. She uses press-moulds to make small component parts that make up her repeat patterns. She builds her vessels from sections of clay that have been imprinted with patterned texture, pushing clay into plaster moulds that have either been carved into or cast with textures, such as textile-printing wood blocks.

Lucy Foakes graduated from University College Falmouth in 2010. She uses a range of processes, including building with coils. Her current body of work revolves around the idea of contemporary canopic jars. Her subject is an irreverent mix of death, Ancient Egypt and present-day celebrity culture. Foakes combines traditional methods and materials with laser-cut plastic and metal components.

Demeter's Prize celebrates the Greek goddess of harvest and the history of the trophy. Foakes fuses ancient iconography with references to contemporary award events: the bold outline of Lady Gaga, resplendent in her meat dress, mimics the stylised hieroglyphic figures of Ancient Egypt. The jar is coil-built in white earthenware, decorated using underglazes and a clear glaze with decals and lustre. The lid of the vessel is layered laser-cut acrylic.

Rebecca Vernon's work is heavily inspired by traditional decorative tableware, of the kind usually used in ceremonial table settings. Drawn to its translucent and stone-like qualities, she works predominantly in porcelain, which is ideal for creating sharp, clean edges and perfect for showing off Vernon's multifaceted surfaces.

Each piece is pinched into its basic form. After being left to stiffen, components are carved, using knives and wood chisels, then pieced together. Some pieces are embellished with clear glaze, blue slip or gold lustre.

Rebecca Vernon, *Coffee Pot*, 2008. Vitrified porcelain, 27 x 18 cm (10½ x 7 in). *Photo: courtesy of the artist*

Sculpting and handbuilding

In Vernon's collection *Too much of a good thing* (2009), her hand-carved decanters, goblets and vanity-table trinkets are assembled in collections alongside other pieces of their kind, or with glass objects collected from charity shops, thrift shops or antique markets.

Sarah Purvey's energetic, sizeable vessels appear to reflect the rhythms and textures of the physical landscape. Influenced by the scale of the furrows, fields, layers and colours of the Wiltshire countryside where she works, there is no doubt that Purvey connects with her surroundings, but her interior landscape and a personal drive to create also propel the work. The stone walls, cut stone roofs and bands of colour of Corsham Court in Wiltshire, UK, where she developed this body of work, have also permeated her work. But, the association is not purely one of aesthetics; she has a deep emotional connection to the place, and this energy and spirit feeds into the physical process of making.

The vessels are constructed from coils of stoneware clay. Surfaces are worked when the clay is still raw and at its most responsive. Purvey draws, cuts and slices using a steel point and a knife. At times, additions of soft clay are worked onto the surfaces. These can be a clay of contrasting colour, such as black onto crank or vice versa. Slips are added on top of the initial drawing, with the brush dragging the surface and moving raw clay across the form. Constant rotation on the banding wheel during this activity means the pieces don't have a front or back, but are created in the round. Some pieces are once-fired, without glaze, while others are brushed with a transparent or vellum glaze. All interiors are left unglazed.

Purvey's process is energised, reactive and intuitive. Whilst highly physical, it also fulfils a meditative function. For Purvey each piece is imbued with the fleeting thoughts and emotions that arise during the making process.

RIGHT: Sarah Purvey, *Landscape Series – Rhythm*, 2012. Crank vessel with slips, 60 x 43 x 28 cm (23½ x 17 x 11 in). *Photo: John Taylor.*

Notes
[1] Natasha Daintry in *Breaking the Mould, New Approaches to Ceramics*, Black Dog Publishing, London, 2007.
[2] Edmund de Waal, *The Pot Book*, Phaidon, London, 2011.

The vessel

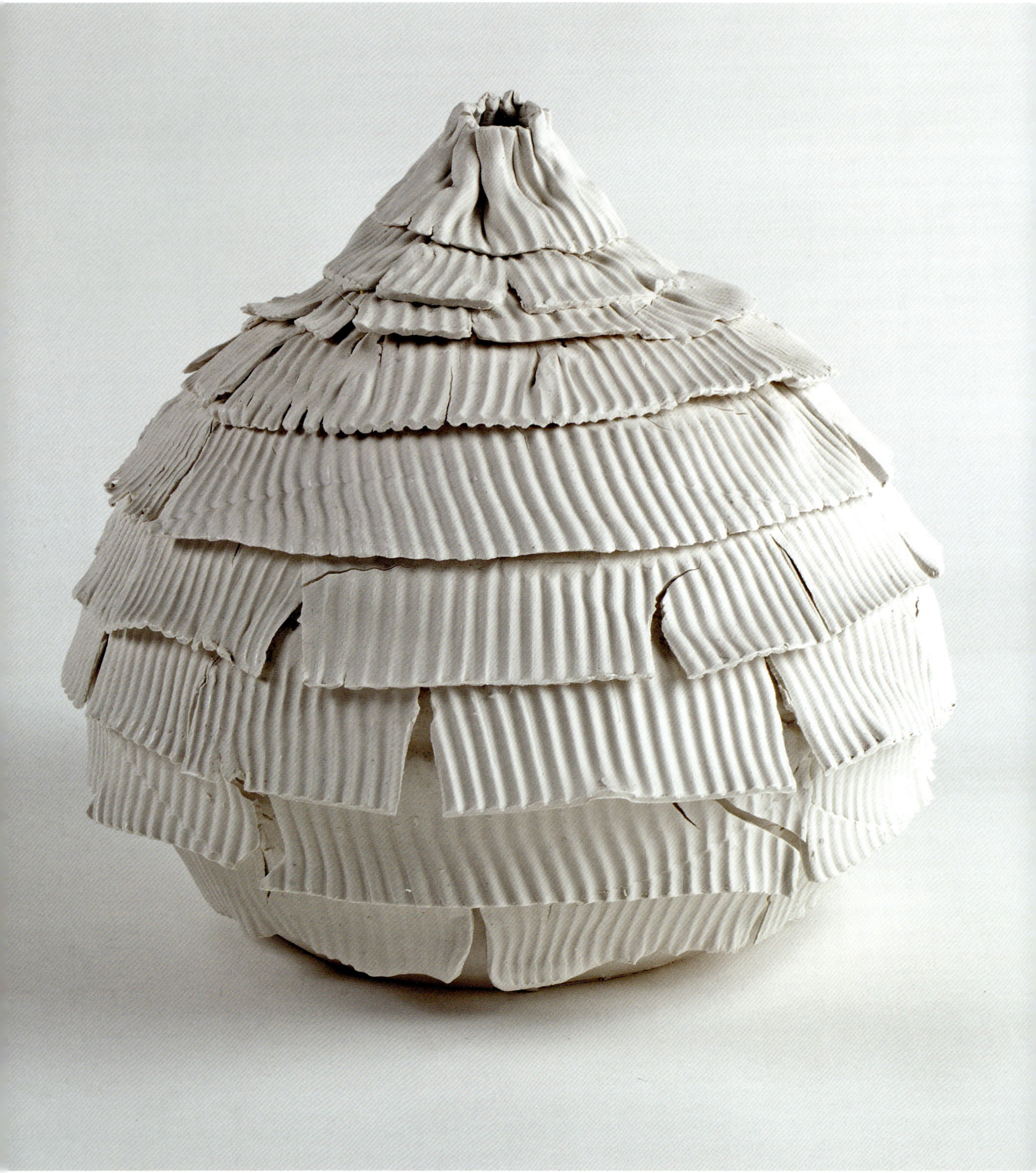

4 Surface treatments

'There are many contemporary artists who use ceramic surface not because of its self-referential possibilities, and not because it occupies three-dimensional space or deals with "volume", but because using slip, underglaze, lustre, onglaze enamel and glazes gives an outstanding palette with which to paint, draw and print.'[1] Paul Scott

Working the surface of a hand-formed structure can be a simple extension of the handbuilding process. There are methods that allow the clay itself to provide texture, decoration and colour, without relying heavily on additional materials or equipment.

Techniques for manipulating the clay surface are as ancient as the methods of construction, possibly older. In fact, the two are indivisible – you can't touch the clay without leaving a trace. Those first finger prints in soft, moist clay inevitably sparked an array of marks, patterns and tactile treatments achievable by the hands alone.

The ancient Mesopotamians used clay tablets for their Cuneiform script, the oldest writing system. Cuneiform is from the Latin *cunes*, meaning 'wedge'. The marks were inscribed using a reed stylus, which resulted in the characteristic wedged shapes in the clay. These tablets demonstrate perfectly the beauty and possibilities of bare clay. From these humble beginnings have grown an increasingly elaborate assortment of methods for enhancing the surface of the clay.

LEFT: Nathalie Khayat, *Seed 5*, 2011. Unglazed porcelain, 31 x 36 cm (12¼ x 14¼ in). *Photo: Elie Bekhazi.*

RIGHT: Makiko Hastings, *Lilypad*, 2012. Pierced unglazed porcelain, 22 cm (8¾ in). *Photo: Makiko Hastings.*

Sculpting and handbuilding

In the 21st century, ceramic surfaces can be incredibly complex locations; many artists load their surfaces with a range of slips, pigments and glazes, using multiple firings, bringing the materials to life. Others continue the traditions of working with the properties of the clay, preserving the belief that the surface doesn't have to be multilayered to engage the eye and successfully excite the hand.

This chapter gives an overview of ceramic surfaces, beginning with the more straightforward, hands-on techniques. This is a huge area for ceramicists and regrettably there is little room to cover it in depth here, but there is a wealth of information and resources available on this subject. As with the artist case studies throughout this book, this chapter should be used as a starting point for further research.

Surface and context

Surface can be a touchy subject for ceramic artists. In the literal sense, some work is made to be touched and experienced by the hands, but there is also the trickier subject of terminology, where the surface 'resides', and which side of the debate you identify with. Is the surface decorated, a term associated with the continuation of ceramic traditions and one which can imply that surface treatment is a veneer sitting on top of the clay structure? Or is it painted, a term more aligned with fine art practices, that can take you into an altogether different contextual territory?

Irrelevant as this may seem when you are starting out, it can be worth considering questions like these as you begin your explorations. They can help you identify artists and approaches that inspire you, and forming an understanding of why and how techniques have evolved can give you the ammunition you need to unpick the traditions, should you wish to.

Elke Sada, *Capriccio XL Bowl*, 2011. White earthenware, 31 cm (12¼ in) wide.
Photo: Michael Wurzbach.

Using clay to add texture and colour

The ancient tradition of burnishing leatherhard clay emerged as a means of sealing clay before the advent of glaze technology. Burnishing compacts the clay particles, making the object water-resistant, while also giving the surface a sheen. Ensure the clay is dry enough, but not too dry, and using a spoon, polished pebble, or similar smooth object, work in a circular motion across the surface of your object; the finer the clay, the smoother the resulting surface will be. Coarser clays can be sprayed with slip to achieve a fine surface. Allow the slip to dry and then burnish.

Impressing objects into the clay slab or directly onto the built form can result in some inventive surfaces and effects. Clay is extremely responsive to touch and is a superb material for gathering textures and fine detail. Anything can be used – a thumbnail, bottle-tops, cutlery, letter stamps, woodworking tools, electronic components, organic matter. Hand-made stamps for impressing a particular texture or shape can be made in clay and used when dry (without firing) or when bisque-fired. A roulette (a tool with a cylindrical roller head fitted with an impressed pattern) can be rolled across the clay surface to give a continuous pattern.

By adding texture, you are disrupting the flat surface and creating a landscape of peaks and troughs. These textures and marks may complete your piece and you may want to leave the work unglazed. If you decide to use colour or glaze, this landscape can be further accentuated by, for example, brushing, sponging or pouring on slip or glaze, or rubbing in oxides. Glaze will pool in the dips, high points will reveal the clay, and oxides will pick out the patterns.

Inlaying is an effective way of adding contrasting clay. For intricate lines and detail, incising the clay with a fine tool is best. Use a metal tool to cut a design into the leatherhard clay then, using a brush, fill the lines with slip of a contrasting colour.

Manuel Canu impressing a pattern in an extruded form as part of his floor installation, 2011. *Photo: Stine Jespersen.*

Elke Sada's studio: Sada works on a plaster bat to create her surfaces. *Photo: Dennis Conrad.*

Keep adding layers of slip until it sits proud of the clay surface. Allow each layer to dry before applying the next. Once dry, scrape back the excess with a metal kidney, revealing the original design.

To make a design with wider marks and lines, inlay using soft clay. With your fingertips, press the clay into the leatherhard surface and allow it to dry. Scrape back with a metal kidney if desired. Another method is to roll contrasting clays into the clay surface, effectively collaging with clay. Inlaying will work with all clays, but white clays and porcelain are best for vivid colours.

Clay shrinks at different rates so if you want a clean, incised mark with no gaps, make sure to mix any slips using the same clay body as the object you are inlaying. If you want to push this process and cultivate cracks, distortions and shrinkage, then experiment with different clay combinations.

Sprigging is a technique associated with Wedgwood and 18th-century ceramic production. Traditionally it involves producing small reliefs to attach to the side of functional or decorative wares by pressing soft clay into carved plaster or small slip moulds. Sprigging can be done effectively without making a mould; instead, found objects can be used to mould clay. Anything that clay can be pressed into and coaxed out of while remaining intact will work. Sprigs can also be made by hand: roll a slab of clay until it is really thin, cut your shape from the clay, allow it to stiffen to leatherhard, then attach with the cross-hatching and slip method previously explained.

Surface treatments

ABOVE LEFT: Jenny Southam applying slip to a composition when leatherhard. *Photo: Kate & Josie Southam.*

ABOVE RIGHT: Makiko Hastings, applying sgraffito pattern on *Mazekoze* slab plate. *Photo: Makiko Hastings.*

The versatility of slip

Slip – liquid clay – is a stalwart of the potter's studio. It is versatile, effective and easy to use. Different slips are used for different purposes. Engobes give a vitreous glaze finish, terra sigillata results in a shiny coating when fired low, crackle slips craze at a certain temperature, and smooth, thick slip mixed with 40-45 per cent water is used for casting. A basic slip made from 1 kg (2lb) ball clay and 2 litres (1¾ pints) of water is ideal for applying to most clay bodies. An array of coloured slips can be made by adding stains and oxides. Slip for painting is generally more watery than casting slip, but the thickness can be adjusted to your requirements.

There are many techniques that utilise the qualities of slip, some already touched on in this chapter. Slip can be painted, poured, dipped, marbled and trailed. Its application range is not unlike paint; you can apply slip washes much like watercolour, or build up thick layers of textured slip similar to layered acrylic. You can rework, re-wet, over-paint and scrape back as you would on canvas. If you work directly onto wet clay, as Sarah Purvey does (p. 74), then the clay body itself becomes part of the palette, along with the slips. This is where ceramic materials come into their own.

Sgraffito involves scratching or incising into clay and is most commonly used to reveal the clay body through a contrasting slip. The piece is coated with slip and then a design is cut through to reveal the clay underneath. The slip can be incised when first applied or when dry, or at all stages in between; each will result in a slightly different effect.

Resists and stencils offer great scope for building up the surface with slip. Used individually or in combination, substances and materials such as wax, latex, paper, open-weave textiles, tape and organic matter can be used to draw or collage the design. Once the design has been drawn out or applied to the clay, brush over, sponge, flick or splatter the slip across the surface.

Colouring the clay body

Staining the clay before building offers a range of possibilities. Stains or oxides can be used as a colourant. Commercial stains provide strong colours and a wide spectrum can be achieved. Staining is most accurately carried out when the clay is in dry form. A white clay body will give the strongest results, but it is worth experimenting with different clay bodies to see what results occur.

Agateware is patterned work made from combinations of coloured clays. There is huge scope for variation. Different clay bodies can be coloured and combined, or the same body of clay stained various colours. Individual colours can be layered to make strips of multicoloured clay, then rolled, shaped, cut and combined to make a kaleidoscope of pattern.

Working with glazes

Glazing is a huge subject and an art form in itself. While many ceramicists dedicate their working lives to exploring and developing glazes, others stick to one or two reliable glazes that meet their requirements. A glaze can be the final surface that brings everything under it to life, or it can provide the solitary colour and texture. It can be combined with other glazes and materials to great effect.

Below are some basic guidelines for glazing. There are many specialist glaze resources available if you want to investigate further.

- Experimenting with the raw materials can be fascinating and frustrating. Either way it is a useful skill to learn. It is all about trial and error, so it is vital to track and record the research you do. There are so many variables – clay type, glaze recipe, application techniques, application thickness, firing cycle, etc. Even if you are using ready-made glazes it is still important to record your process and results.

Makiko Hastings' glaze test tiles. *Photo: Makiko Hastings.*

Surface treatments

- Mixing dry glaze ingredients can be hazardous so always wear a mask and, in many cases, surgical gloves when you weigh and prepare your glaze.
- To mix your own glazes you will need accurate scales, a spoon to measure out the glaze powder, mixing bowls, lidded airtight containers for storage, sieves (80 and 100 mesh), a stick or wooden spatula for stirring, a stiff bristled brush for pushing the glaze material through the sieve, a rubber kidney to collect and push any remaining stubborn glaze through the sieve, and a permanent marker pen to record the glaze details on your storage container. Glaze will keep for a long time if stored properly.
- Successful glazing relies heavily on accuracy at the mixing stage. Most raw ingredients look the same so it is useful to work with a list of the ingredients that you can tick off as you add them to the mix. This will prevent any confusion if you are distracted.
- Traditionally, glaze is added after the bisque firing, when other colours have already been applied. Many potters and ceramicists use this approach. Other ceramicists, including myself, work with glaze materials (combined with slips and underglaze) directly on to the raw clay. Glaze can be added when the clay is wet or leatherhard or at any stage in between. The appeal of single firing is the compliancy of the wet clay canvas in conjunction with these other ceramic materials.

Other materials

Treatments for ceramic surfaces have developed markedly in recent years. Although glazing remains a 'wait and see' process, with testing and practice you will learn how to control what happens. There are many materials you can use for pattern, colour and texture that are much more 'what you see is what you get'. Painting with commercial underglazes, drawing with ceramic pencils, and crayons are good ways to get to grips with ceramic materials as their application colours remain or improve after firing.

Makiko Hastings drawing on *Rakugaki* dish with ceramic pencil. *Photo: Makiko Hastings.*

Sculpting and handbuilding

Another way to decorate the ceramic surface is to apply print materials. It is easy to buy decals (ceramic transfers) made from your own designs but there are many other processes to explore. UK artist and author Paul Scott is a leading proponent of ceramics and print, and has done much to expand this field with his research and publications on the subject.

Jacqueline Leighton Boyce lives and works on Exmoor. It is this location that provides a rich source of inspiration for her illustrative vessels: 'My work is fairly personal and solitary, and displays a simple and sometimes romantic narrative taken from regularly walking in and around Exmoor.' It is important to her that the clay 'shows itself'. She works her forms and surfaces to demonstrate the rawness and immediacy of her materials. Her pieces are coil-built and she works primarily with terracotta clay, firing to 1080°C (1976°F). Each piece is usually fired three times. Although her surfaces are multi-layered with lustre, gorged marks, drawings, underglaze, slips and glaze, the clay itself is still visible. Between the layers of colour, we can glimpse the terracotta; this serves as a reminder of the physical landscape

Claire Loder, *Looking for a Pattern*, 2010. Slab-built with slips, underglaze, glaze and plastic spectacles. Single-fired, height: 30 cm (11¾ in). *Photo: John Taylor.*

Surface treatments

Jacqueline Leighton Boyce, *I gazed across the valley but I could not see the stag*, 2011. Red terracotta clay, slip, underglaze, lustre, 28 x 32 cm (11 x 12½ in). *Photo: courtesy of the artist.*

of the moor, upon which unfold the narratives with which Leighton Boyce encircles her vessels. Poetic titles such as *I gazed across the valley but I could not see the stag* or *At last I saw the river flow again* perpetuate the myth and mysticism of this unique landscape. Her vessels are painted in the round, inside and out, with no front or back, so no view is the same.

Note
[1] Paul Scott, *Painted Clay: Graphic Arts and the Ceramic Surface*, A&C Black, London, 2001.

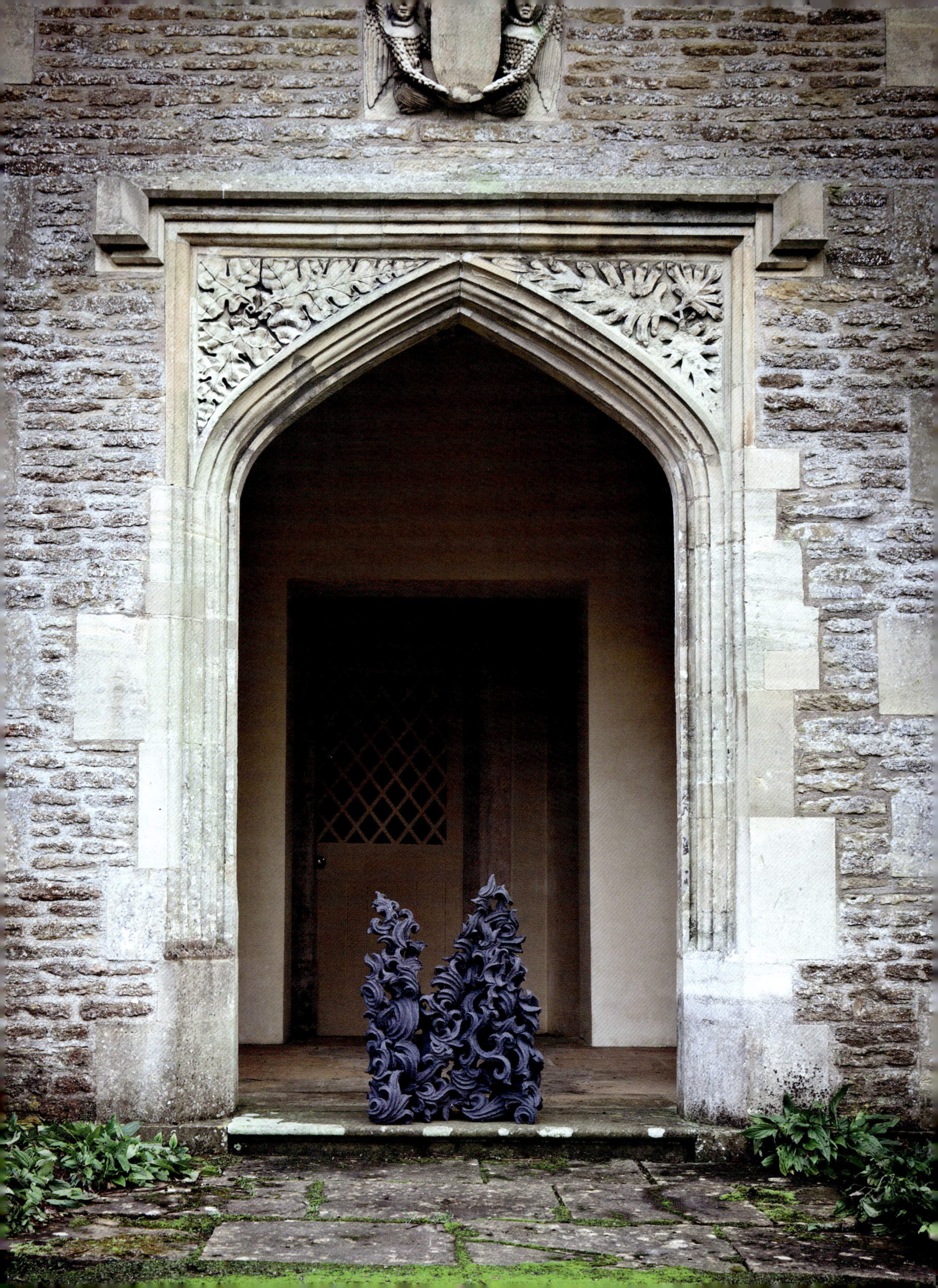

5 Sculptural approaches

'It is important to endure the disasters and difficulties; fragility is part of the tension that can make interesting art.'[1] Fenella Elms

The technical and practical considerations of making sculptural pieces using handbuilding methods are as varied as the diversity of works that fall under this loose definition. Sculptural ceramics is a very broad church, covering anything from small-scale figurines to ambitious abstract forms.

Clay used to be a staging post for casting in bronze, a perfunctory, practical material. The elevation of clay to a sculptural material in its own right has greatly added to the sculptor's vocabulary. Clay is readily available, adaptable, scalable and highly responsive to touch. It can be contradictory – fragile and robust, transitory and permanent, rarefied and relaxed. It can mimic and mock.

There are many different kinds of practitioners currently sculpting with clay. Artists such as Leiko Ikemura, Brendan Huntley and Klara Kristalova draw on the figurative sculptural tradition but exploit the material qualities of clay and ceramic substances. Others, like Richard Long and Andrew Goldsworthy, working within the landscape, are involved hand and body with clay in its most visceral form – mud. They make us look afresh at the simple tactility of the substance.

Born 1964 in Stoke-on-Trent, England, **Stephen Bird** now divides his life and work between Australia and Scotland. Ostensibly slip-cast and drawing reference from the 18th and 19th century Staffordshire tradition of the figurine, Bird's pieces are, in fact, hand-formed. He says of his work: 'Exploring the fine line between what is comic and what is tragic and working in hybrid mediums, which are not quite painting and not quite sculpture, has always interested me. There is something more authentic to me about the grey area of the painted form, which seems to have the potential to reveal something of what it is to be human.'

Bird refers to his collaged figures as 'painter's sculptures'. Although his work has strong narrative content, Bird's main focus is the tension between the structure of the work and the painted surface and is more about formal concerns of drawing on a three-dimensional plane.

All works are handbuilt or press-moulded and constructed from a variety of clays. Sometimes Bird uses a press-moulded component to build up forms, rather like working with Lego. Works are painted raw with slips, under glazes and oxides, and bisque-fired to 1000°C (1832°F). Engobes, clear and tin glazes are applied and are often over-painted with oxides and underglaze and fired to 1115°C (2039°F). He often over-paints with on-glaze enamels. Through these layers, the colours are modified until the correct harmony and tone is achieved.

LEFT: Jo Taylor, *Black Form*, 2012. Black grogged clay, 75 x 64 x 25 cm (29½ x 25 x 9¾ in). *Photo: Andy Rose.*

Sculpting and handbuilding

LEFT: Stephen Bird, *Staffordshire Psycho with blunderbuster*, 2011. Clay pigment glaze, 32 x 20 x 16 cm (12½ x 7¾ x 6¼ in). *Photo: Artist and Rex Irwin, art dealer.*

RIGHT: Christy Keeney, *Mother and Child*, 2008. Finely-grogged clay mixed with flax. Slips, stains, oxides, fired to 1160°C (2120°F), 45 x 17 x 11 cm (17¾ x 6½ x 4¼ in). *Photo: Christy Keeney.*

Bird subverts contemporary narratives, exploring themes as broad as politics, religion and the everyday. His experiences working in countries such as Thailand, India, Scotland and Australia are evident in his work, which directly references a global view of archetypal themes of love, death, birth and life, with an element of humour, social comment and political satire. 'The actual surface of the work is quite irreverent and my concern with the tension between the structure of the work and the painted surface has been a thread running through my work for the past 20 years,' Bird says. 'The process of assemblage may fuse all the components into a unified work, but the way in which they are painted maintains their individual identities and threatens to pull the whole thing apart.'

Over the years Bird has worked with many other mediums, including painting, drawing and cardboard construction. When he began making ceramics in 1996, he saw it as a place where all those other activities came together. Bird has never stopped painting but finds that, as ceramics is a very demanding material, every time he opens the kiln he always feels as though it is not quite right. 'If I ever get it right, I may quite well move onto something else.'

Christy Keeney studied ceramics at the Royal College of Art, London, and is well known for his slab-built figurative work. The seed for this work first came from an encounter with Picasso's small cardboard cut-outs at a 1980s retrospective. Since then, destruction and construction have been an element in Keeney's work. Drawing and sculpture combine in his pieces, as Keeney's faces and figures take form with drawn details in the wet clay.

In the last few years Keeney has turned to painting. He feels that ceramics and painting use different parts of his creative brain. Ceramics are tied up with process whereas painting offers greater spontaneity. When painting, Keeney layers up the paint, over-painting and working the surface until the environment and atmosphere are right. Once achieved, he adds his figure or figures. Painting allows Keeney to set the scene for his subjects, and it's this that appeals to him, as ultimately this luxury is unavailable when producing his sculptures. There is continuity with his sculptures – figuration is the focus; the theme of isolation evident in so much of Keeney's ceramics work remains; the drawn line is still significant; and his palette is consistent. The two strands of his work are interwoven but serve different functions for the artist.

Sculpting and handbuilding

Claire Loder's – my own – heads are full of ideas, a union of modern day concerns, wordplay, outsider influence and the interior world. They are a combination of intuitive construction, amorphous tactility and off-kilter form. My subjects are static, but traces of cogitation are suggested in the expressive use of glaze. My stony faces are lighter than they appear, the hollow interiors a repository for the thoughts, feelings and emotions of both the subject and the viewer. Through the titles of my pieces, rudimentary forms become a vehicle for my personal interests and concerns – the depiction of melancholy, innuendo, the search for quiet and an array of 21st-century anxieties.

Each piece is slab-built and single-fired. As soon as the structure will stand, I start to paint the surface. Using a combination of fine detail and expressive strokes, the wet clay becomes part of my palette. The ongoing *Glad to wear glasses* series, started in 2010, was my first use of found objects and materials added after firing.

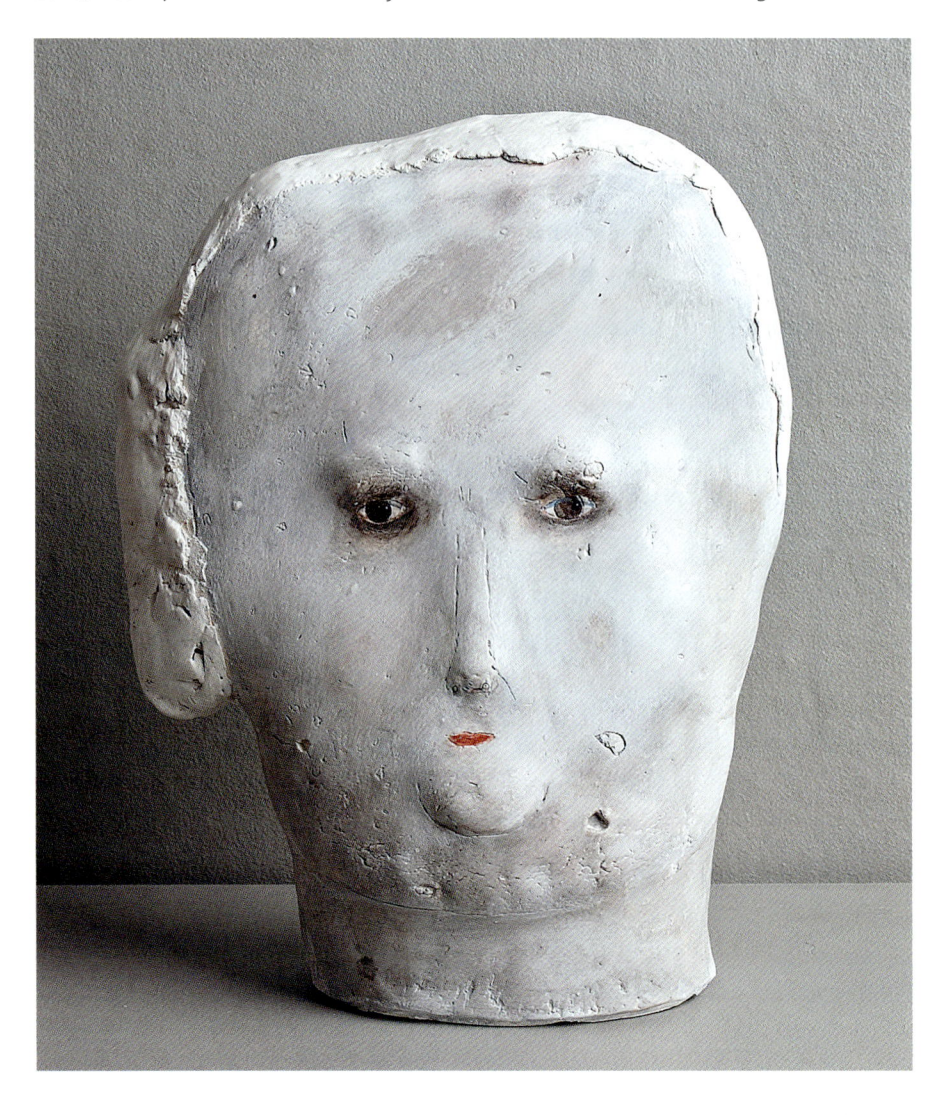

Claire Loder, *Second Thoughts*, 2009. White earthenware, slip, underglazes, matt glaze, single-fired, height: 28 cm (11 in). *Photo: John Taylor.*

Kaori Tatebayashi, *Blouse*, 2009. Slab construction, 58 x 63 x 6 cm (22¾ x 24¾ x 2¼ in). *Photo: Julian Haynes.*

Kaori Tatebayashi makes beautifully-observed everyday objects using slab-building techniques. Her objects have a stillness and poeticism that is captured in the way she writes about what she does: 'I use clay as a device to make fragments of time visible. I want to preserve the intimate and transient recollections of our lives and seal them in the clay, like a fern petrified into a fossil. Firing changes soft, malleable clay into hard, breakable ceramic. As clay loses its organic life in the firing, it allows time to become encased. The nature of fired clay incorporates both fragility and permanence, and it is this that enables the material to record elusive things like memory.'

As a young child, Tatebayashi's family moved from one place to another due to her parents' work, losing her possessions and treasured objects along the way. Learning to focus on the memories of childhood rather than those unreliable objects is what underpins Tatebayashi's work. 'I trace everyday objects in clay, like an old pair of shoes, a girl's camisole or a discarded box of buttons – the sort of bits and pieces you might have owned once but have forgotten all about. Through looking at my work, you are led back into those tiny, quiet recesses of your past.'

Sculpting and handbuilding

Sculptural approaches

LEFT: Sophie Woodrow, *Shell*, 2011. Porcelain – pinched, coiled, modelled, 14 cm (5½ in). *Photo: Benjamin Dowden.*

Sophie Woodrow was born in Bristol, where she now has her studio. She studied ceramics at Falmouth College of Art. Her porcelain animalistic sculptures display a dreamlike hotchpotch of real and invented characteristics. Starting with a coil-built form, Woodrow then incises and impresses the clay to achieve delicately textured surfaces.

Repeatedly drawn to images of nature, she uses animals to reflect and explore the relationship between the human and animal world. Woodrow has looked particularly at our continually shifting theories of evolution. A particular source of inspiration is the enormous misinterpretations of geological evidence made by the Victorians. Woodrow's sculptures are not visitors from other worlds, but the 'might-have-beens' of this world.

Jenny Southam lives and works in Devon. She works in the medium of terracotta, specialising in individual handbuilt figurative sculptures, most of which reference her fascination with Etruscan tomb sculptures and Staffordshire mantelpiece figures.

The sculptures explore mythic and domestic themes, and many are inspired by working in the garden. They are informed by the patterns and rituals that we construct to keep our world sane and smooth; for example, by making beds, feeding the birds and the seasonal cycle of planting seeds. The figures are enraptured by their immediate and intimate connection to each other and to the natural world. The works are celebratory, although in a quiet and contemplative way, the oxides and the slips decorating the sculptures used in an intuitive manner to echo the works' emotional rhythm.

The exploration of scale is an important part of Southam's practice. Some sculptures are only a few inches high, whilst others are imposing figures at two feet tall.

Jenny Southam, *Couple coming across a monolith in the forest*, 2011. Slab-building and hand-modelling, decorated with slips, 24 x 28 cm (9½ x 11 in). *Photo: John Melville.*

Sculpting and handbuilding

Stephanie Quayle, *Fox on Bucket* (detail), 2011. Grogged terracotta, 50 x 35 x 30 cm (19½ x 13¾ x 11¾ in). *Photo: courtesy of the artist.*

Stephanie Quayle is a sculptor working in clay. A fascination for 'animal-ness' and pursuing what it is like to be animal drives her making process. Living on a farm, immersed in the countryside environment and spending time in the wildernesses of Belize, Laos and Bangladesh are raw, vital experiences that inform Qualye's work, as does her conviction that, although no longer able to recognise our place in nature, human souls are inescapably bound up in the natural world.

Direct and energetic in Qualye's hands, the clay becomes inhabited rather than a mere image of the subject. Her large-scale, handbuilt animals always begin with intensive drawings, predominantly from life, getting to know every characteristic, muscle and mannerism. This fresh, energetic pace of drawing can then be transferred to vigorously handbuilt sculptures, which capture the essence and energy of the animals, confronting the animal before and within us. The heavily-grogged clays allows an expressive, fast, direct and uninterrupted way of capturing the drawn line in space, whilst retaining the primitive, earthy texture of the mud-like material and allowing space for the clay to just be.

Fenella Elms' 'co-operative bodies of indiscernibly shifting components' are made with porcelain, chosen for its hardness when thin and its glowing, translucent quality. Small pieces, strips and edges are aligned into intricate structures and textures. Nearly all the work begins as slip, which she makes up to different consistencies to pour onto plaster.

RIGHT: Fenella Elms, *Moules 3*, 2010. Stained porcelain, 65 x 65 x 2 cm (25½ x 25½ x ¾ in). *Photo: courtesy of the artist.*

Sculptural approaches

Sculpting and handbuilding

There is no particular appeal in just one single component for Elms; the interaction of similar but separate components and the challenge of working with the material drives her work. 'The technical challenges appeal because I thrill to see what the materials can do and I find that the problems give rise to new directions with making, handling and firing, as well as mounting and presenting the work. I like to see evidence of the building and firing process in the finished piece: the joins, the tears and shifts. Timing and rhythm, touch and feeling are crucial to facilitate the building.'

David Hicks is an artist living and working in North Carolina. Drawn to the 'collective power of things', Hicks makes work consisting of grouped objects or repeated motifs that are organic in origin. He is inspired by the organic forms common to the American landscape and his upbringing in an area dominated by agriculture.

Hicks' wall pieces resemble harvested objects, which Hicks sees as 'unearthed or decaying'. There is a sense of hyper nature in his forms, especially with recent, glossy works, that lends the forms a heightened fecundity, reinforced by their large size. The scale of his work is inevitable, says Hicks, given his own sizable frame and the necessity to work in an unhindered way.

Hicks combines many handbuilding techniques, including coiling, pinching, slab-building and extruding. For many of his wall pieces, he hangs his collections off steel cable or combines terracotta with wood, plastics, glass, bronze and plaster. For Hicks, surface is all about layers of texture and colour, and the possibilities and connotations keep him experimenting. His wall pieces usually have dry, earthy tones, layers of clay and glaze making up the strata of these pieces. By contrast, his single objects are coated in wet, dripping glaze that signifies an organic form 'in the prime of its existence'.

RIGHT: David Hicks, *Still Life (lavender)*, 2011. Coiled and pinched terracotta, with coloured slip and steel, 127 x 41 x 28 cm (50 x 16 x 11 in). *Photo: David Hicks*.

Note
[1] Fenella Elms, quoted in Fielding, A, July 2011 'Swirling Movements and Illusions of Growth', *Ceramic Review*, Issue 250.

Sculptural approaches

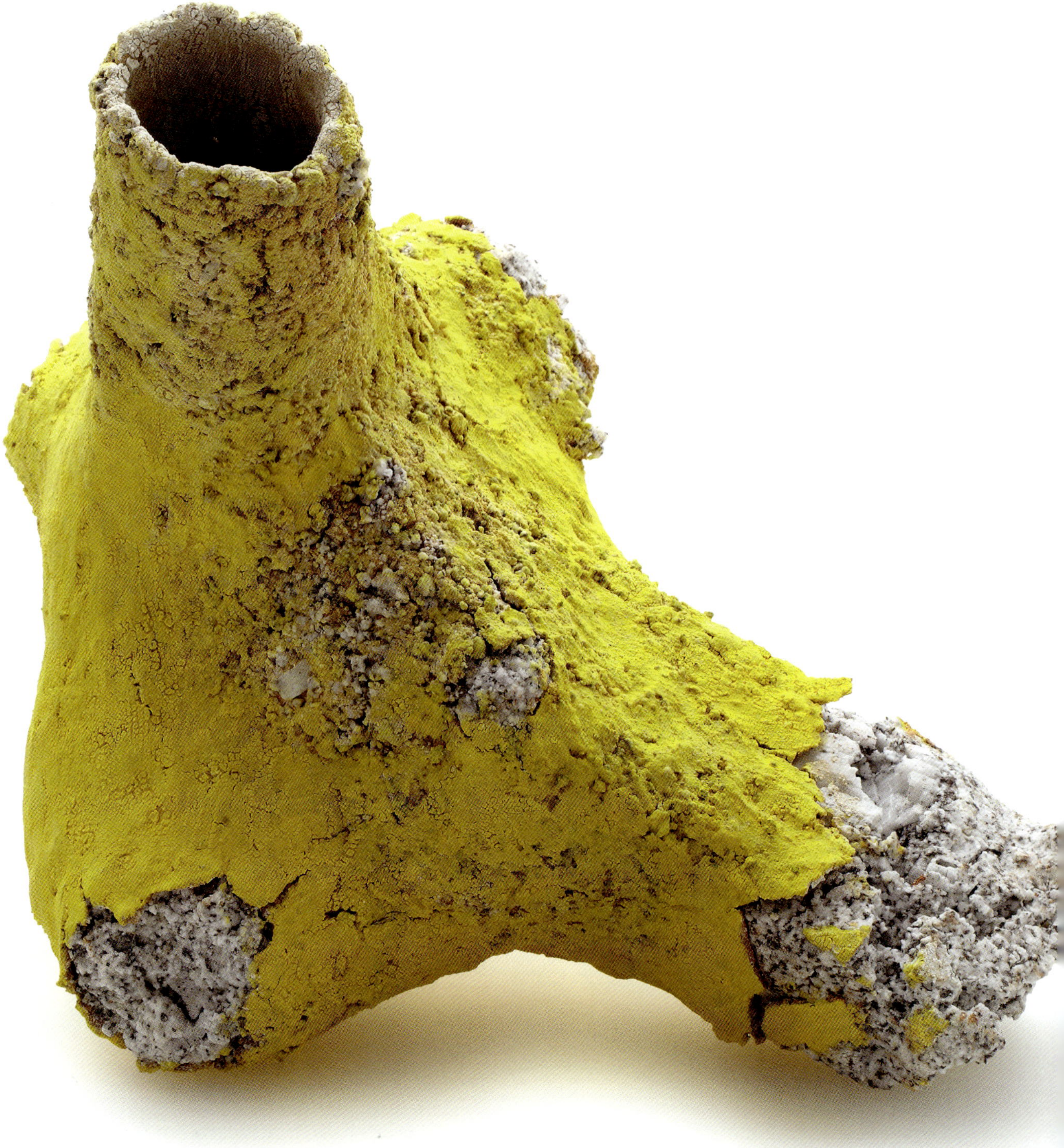

6 Combining techniques and materials

'Strangeness is something we need. It is disruptive and mind-opening.'[1]
Gillian Lowndes

In Britain, after the Second World War, new thinking about the possibilities of expression offered by clay began to surface. No longer bound by traditional ideas about materials, restraint and quiet beauty, which were tenets of the Leach philosophy, the modern ceramics movement began to appropriate ideas and techniques from the world of fine art. The strict adherence to single-method construction was abandoned in favour of a mixed build approach, and explorations combining different clays, and clay with other non-ceramic materials, gained credence.

Combining techniques

Once you have mastered – or indeed, as a *means* to mastering – the basic handbuilding techniques, it is useful, desirable and often necessary to combine building methods. One of the most common examples of combined techniques is using a thumb pot or pinch pot as a base and then extending the walls with coils. A pinch pot can just as easily be extended with slabs, pinched pellets or torn segments. A thickly-coiled structure can be carved into, or sculpted elements and hand-modelled pieces can be attached to a slab-built box – there are numerous permutations. Bonnie Smith, for example, uses various techniques to build each piece, often starting with a solid block (see p.40) then continuing with another method. When combining building methods make sure all the joins are thoroughly sealed, as there may be variations in thickness between parts of the piece, which can lead to cracks – again the drying has an important part to play here. You can alter the drying times by unwrapping thicker areas so they can catch up with thinner sections.

Combining clays

Combining various types of clay in one piece of work is another fascinating area of exploration. Each clay has specific attributes and behaves in a different way when fired. Fractures, cracks and breakages can be encouraged and controlled, to some extent, through experimentation and record keeping. Combining clays with different shrinkage rates will bring intriguing results. You can also combine different coloured

LEFT: Aneta Regel Deleu, *Metamorphosis*, 2011/2012. Stoneware clay and volcanic rock, height: 30 cm (11¾ in). *Photo: Sylvain Deleu.*

Anne Mercedes, *Soleil Eclaté*, 2012. Porcelain, stoneware, feldspars. Fired in reduction at cone 9 (1280°C/2336°F), 45 x 40 x 27 cm (17¾ x 15¾ x 10½ in). *Photo: Sussie Ahlburg.*

clays, or play with variations in viscosity. Try building with a combination of fine clays and textures, or pouring porcelain slip over a crank-clay form. The influential UK ceramic artist Ewen Henderson (1934–2000) worked in this way. He perfected a patchwork technique for his asymmetric vessels, combining various clays such as porcelain, bone china and terracotta. Sculptor Anne Mercedes also combines various clays and minerals. Her sculptures capture a moment of movement and disintegration, a physical action that signifies Mercedes' philosophical interest in evolution. After firing she grinds or carves, or adds other media.

Additions

Various substances and materials can be integrated or added to the clay, before and after firing. Caroline Achaintre drapes, tears, hangs and textures the clay surface, adding leather, steel and various other items, post-firing, in her darkly comic sculptures. The German ceramicist Gertraud Mohwald (1929–2002) added boldly collaged fragments to the clay. Mohwald made robust and muscular sculptures using large sections of pre-fired ceramics to form her semi-abstract faces and torsos. Fragments of crockery can be used, much like collage, and there are many contemporary ceramicists who adopt this method. If you want to combine clay and wire there are various wires that withstand the firing process and others that either burn out completely, leaving a wire-

Combining techniques and materials

shaped void or some sort of trace. The action of burning away a particular material can be used – for example, rice rolled into the clay surface will burn out, leaving small indentations. Experiment with a range of organic matter or inert substances to see what surfaces or texture they create.

A wide range of other material can be added after firing. You may need to plan how to attach the material before the work is fired, making the necessary holes or joining point. You will also need to consider clay shrinkage if you are attaching a specific substance.

The added complexity of combining techniques, especially if you have a particularly intricate structure, can be helped by planning and drawing first.

Aneta Regel Deleu graduated from the Royal College of Art in 2006. Her sculptural pieces combine her preoccupation with the natural world versus the human-made world. Regel fuses ceramic materials with organic rock and is interested in the physical tension between these opposing substances when forced together in the kiln. Her starting points are the elements in the landscape of her northern Polish upbringing, most notably the large stones of myth and legend, created by the glaciers' retreat. The result is often unearthly, amplified by dazzling surface colours.

Regel produces hollow and solid sculptures. Abstract as they are, they still emit a visceral and bodily energy. This is Regel's intention. 'I want to put life into form, arrest motion, capture energy and rhythm. Not simply a shape, but a feeling, a smell, energy or an emotion,' she says. Often Regel displays several pieces together, setting

Claire Loder, *Barb*, 2009. White earthenware, slip, underglazes, matt glaze, glasses, broom bristles, single-fired, height: 21 cm (8¼ in). *Photo: John Taylor*.

101

Sculpting and handbuilding

Combining techniques and materials

LEFT: Bonnie Smith, *Heaven and Earth*, 2011. Earthenware, porcelain, glazes, paints, found objects, hand-sculpted and pinched, 46 x 46 cm (18 x 18 in). *Photo: Storm Photo.*

up a beautiful and odd communion between works of differing colours, scales, forms and characteristics.

Bonnie Marie Smith's subject is the figure. Her small-scale sculptures explore her personal experiences, relationships and emotions. Informed by myths, dreams and symbols, she is also guided by the material's response to her touch.

Smith's work is a product of her love affair with clay. There is a tenderness and sensuality in her approach, and her figures are created with affection. 'I love the way clay feels, and I love how directly and immediately it is marked by my touch,' she says. 'It is a very sensual substance to work with, and to me, it feels almost alive. Making ceramic sculpture is for me a process of interacting with the clay. I touch the clay and I watch for interesting things to arise out of that touch.'

Smith uses a range of handbuilding techniques, depending on the scale and form of the work. For smaller works, she often sculpts the figure from solid pieces of clay, which are then hollowed out. Pinching, press-moulding and coiling are then used to make the additional elements. Larger sculptures are often built from coils or pinched forms, which are joined together. Each piece is constructed from earthenware or porcelain clay, with applied glazes, stains and paints and the occasional found object.

Hans Borgonjon's work is about tension: he combines different clays, colours and processes, making sculptures that are large yet fragile. He blends handbuilt elements with slip-casting, and pure white porcelain with the earth tones of terracotta, and his large-as-life sculptures are bold but brittle. The cylinder is often present in Borgonjon's work, either visibly or by suggestion. Smooth casings are the perfect counterweight to his expressive handbuilt elements, as in *Jaws*, 2009 (below).

RIGHT: Hans Borgonjon, *Jaws*, 2009. Porcelain and red earthenware, handbuilt and slip-cast, 24 x 24 x 12 cm (9½ x 9½ x 4¾ in). *Photo: Hans Borgonjon.*

Sculpting and handbuilding

LEFT: Hans Borgonjon, *Microtubuli* in the construction stage, 2011. Coiled, 50 x 50 cm (19½ x 19½ in). *Photo: Hans Borgonjon.*

RIGHT*:* Hans Borgonjon, *Microtubuli XL*, 2009. Red earthenware and stoneware, handbuilt and slip-cast, 50 x 50 cm (19½ x 19½ in). *Photo: Hans Borgonjon.*

Microtubuli (2008–9) is another series of works, based on lattices and networks. Having worked for many years as an intensive care nurse, Borgonjon's work has a distinctly biological, cellular feel. Ropes of clay are constructed, web-like, by hand, using a mould as a former. These rough coils are animate and expressive. The work is not slick, glossy or unemotional; the imperfections produced in this hands-on process communicate the visceral nature of the body.

Much like the physical structure of his lattice pieces, there is a complexity to Borgonjon's work, with overlapping threads and themes. He is concerned with consciousness and personal experience. In a reaction to the virtual world encounters that bombard us, Borgonjon is attempting to communicate the sense of self that is constructed from real world sensations. 'I try to reflect contrasting states of human strength and fragility, simplicity and complexity, and a sense of familiarity and alienation. This is hopefully perceptible in small handheld tactile work to porcelain wall pieces, intricately woven clay vessels and more conceptual and figurative ceramic structures. I make objects playing with light and shadow. I marry clashing techniques and knit contrasting clays in seemingly simple forms.'

Consuelo Seixas Radclyffe combines clay with wire and paper for her narrative sculptures, exploring themes of childhood. Borrowing freely from many traditions, especially her native Brazil, Radclyffe makes figurative ensembles, most commonly depicting children with their imaginary friends. The idea of the imaginary friend lends itself to Radclyffe's technique – it's the perfect vehicle by which to explore mixed media. Radclyffe makes paper clothes for her characters and incorporates found objects such as paperclips. She works with stoneware and paperclay and uses stains and oxides for colouring.

Combining techniques and materials

Consuelo Seixas Radclyffe, *When I was that big …* , 2011. Stoneware, paper, glazes, 35 cm (13¾ in). *Photo: Sussie Ahlburg.*

    Radclyffe explains: 'My characters and stories are formed by the presence of clothing and objects of comfort, moments in the past, playtimes, sibling rivalry, imaginary friends, creating metaphors intimately associated with nostalgia, loss and belonging.'

    Hanne Mannheimer was born in Sweden and completed her MA at the Royal College of Art in 2010 and she is now based in London. Many things go into Mannheimer's work – some solid, others less tangible.

    Here she talks about her making process: 'More often than not, it begins with a found object, like the texture of a thread or the memory of a porcelain figurine. Sometimes the found can be a story, even a few words describing something or a

Combining techniques and materials

feeling that needs to be made in a tactile and fragile material. The combination of the found and made, a tangible object and an abstract idea, is what motivates me the most. This allows the material qualities of the clay to interact with the refined details of the found elements. I love the clumsy, awkward and sometimes ugly qualities that can be found in old and discarded objects with their inherent narratives, suggesting the passing of time.'

Mannheimer works through a lot of her ideas on paper. Some drawings will become ideas for her surfaces, as she experiments with marks, textures, abstraction. Rather than designing three-dimensional forms on paper, she applies her open drawing approach to her work with clay and found objects.

Emma Rodgers has been making and drawing since she was a small child. Her numerous pets, particularly her Siamese cat, were her main source of inspiration. Rodgers is also influenced by her great-grandfather, who was a missionary in Africa and collected a vast array of artefacts from his travels. 'I would often wander to the study,' she says, 'and rummage through his collections of armadillo shells, fossils and tribal carving.'

It's a natural progression from those formative experiences to the works she now produces. Her approach is unsentimental, raw and conveys what she describes as 'agility and latent energy'. Rodgers describes where she starts: 'Once a body of sketches, using quick ink mark-making, charcoals, photographs and film, has been produced, paying particular attention to joints and movement and the finer details of a subject such as face, digits and in some cases behaviour, I can continue to make the piece.'

Hanne Mannheimer, *Untitled (dog)*, 2010. Found object, clay and wire, 10 x 10 cm (4 x 4 in). *Photo: Dominic Tschudin.*

Sculpting and handbuilding

LEFT: Emma Rodgers and Elaine Peto, *Hare Bride from the tales of Brothers Grimm*, 2012. Porcelain and mixed media, 63 x 56 x 38 cm (25 x 22 x 15 in). *Photo: Mills Media.*

Rodgers starts with a thick slab of clay. From this, she sculpts and models her pieces, constructing from the torso outwards, adding limbs and appendages joint by joint. This construction method mimics the real anatomy of the figure and gives Rodgers the flexibility to manipulate each part of her subject's body to position it as she wants. Her knowledge of anatomy comes from hours of observation, sketching and where possible interacting with the animals. Greater understanding of animal anatomy, other than visual documentary, has been achieved by attending animal autopsies.

Rodgers works with a range of materials, mixing clays and mixing ceramic materials with other matter – wire, springs, nails and smashed crockery. She combines stoneware and porcelain, exploiting the effects of their slightly different shrinkage rates. Firing is to 1140°C (2084°F) with a soak of 20 minutes. The firings are repeated to add strength to the piece without a danger of warping.

RIGHT: Emma Rodgers, *The Kneeling Showgirl*, 2003. Porcelain, 20 x16 x15 cm (8 x 6½ x 6 in). *Photo: Steve Barry.*

Combining techniques and materials

Sculpting and handbuilding

LEFT: Emma Rodgers, Crafts Council Firing Up project with the artist and school children in the Wirral, 2011. After firing the ceramic sheep were introduced to the field of sheep to see how they interacted. *Photo: Emma Rodgers.*

In 2011, Rodgers took her mixed media approach into schools, as part of the Crafts Council's Firing Up Scheme, working with the children to help them create handbuilt sculptures of sheep. The sheep were modelled from life, using handbuilding techniques, their surfaces pressed with straw for surface texture and later smoke-fired with materials from the school grounds.

Edith Garcia produces work in series. Using emotive titles such as *Dicen que te quieren* (*They say that they love you*), her over-arching theme is the human condition. Through installation, mixed media, sound and sculpture, she explores ideas around childhood, exploitation, domesticity and the monster within. She builds by hand using ceramic materials, applying drawing, painting and many other techniques while maintaining a distinct style. There are graphic and illustrative aspects to Garcia's output, and much of her work is wall-mounted, bringing into question the traditional plinth-based approach for ceramic artists. This liberation allows a free-flowing narrative to develop between the individual components. Although these individual elements are often domestic in size, the installations as a whole span large wall spaces, illustrating the power of collected objects.

In her *Happy Ugly Scars* series (2009–11), the use of vinyl graphics complements the surface of Garcia's ceramic figures and is a step closer towards directly drawing on the gallery wall. The *Absence + Presence* series (2010) is a pared-down abstraction of the human form. And in the *Loss of Love* pieces (2010), the artist's hands are evident. It's easy to imagine her coaxing these forms from the clay. These delightfully rudimentary pieces seem far removed from the process-heavy earlier series, but the immediacy of the figures still communicates Garcia's trademark disfiguration and unsettling approach.

Note

[1] Gillian Lowndes, catalogue essay on Gillian Lowndes by Alison Britton, *Contemporary Applied Arts*, 1994.

RIGHT: Edith Garcia, *Absence + Presence, In-between*, 2010. Hand-modelled element from multi-media installation. *Photo: courtesy of the artist.*

Combining techniques and materials

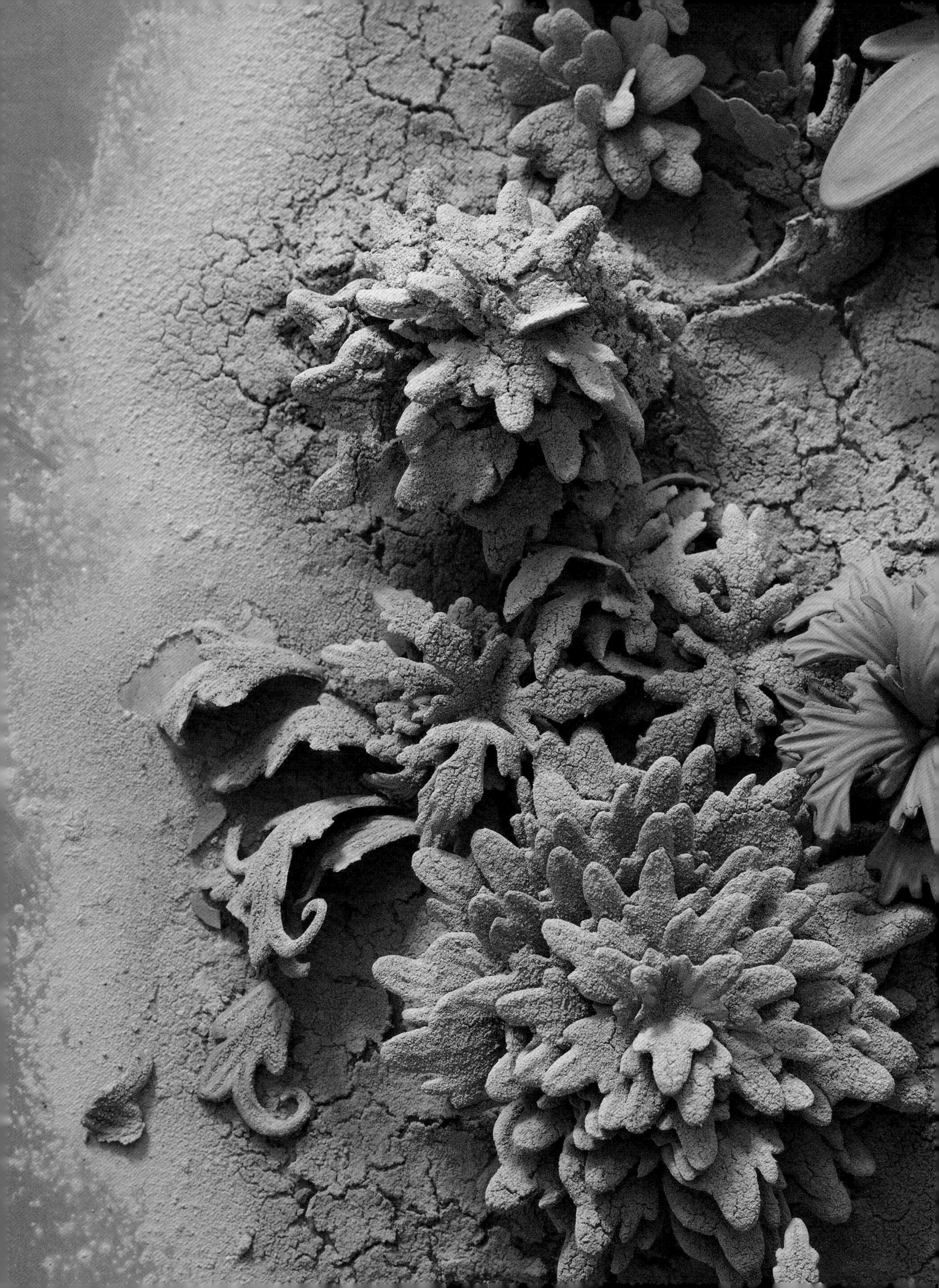

7 Contemporary approaches

'When working with ceramics, I use a large palette of clays and minerals, and the firing is assigned a crucial role: it is expected to disrupt that which I have carefully constructed.'[1] Anne Mercedes

Clay practice in the early 21st century is many things. While debates around art and craft perpetuate, in studios and workshops artists are getting on with the matter in hand: investigating what clay can do. Many artists who push the boundaries of ceramic convention and test material possibilities are using handbuilding and sculptural methods to make real their ideas.

Clare Twomey, in her essay in *Breaking The Mould*, states that: 'Investigative, non-conventional approaches to clay are endemic of our time.'[2] Twomey is one of several innovative artists, along with others such as Phoebe Cummings, Philip Li and Shay Church, who experiment with the possibilities and properties of unfired clay manipulated by hand-forming methods. For some, it is the focus of their work; for others it is just one of many approaches employed as part of a diverse practice using many materials and techniques. Clay may satisfy one part of their creative vision, while other processes, for example, drawing, painting, collage, writing or animation, fulfil other functions allowing them to experiment with the material qualities of other mediums, work in a different scale or operate in other markets.

It's no coincidence, but it is a paradox, that new territory is being broken with this back-to-basics approach. Raw clay allows artists to be intuitive, expressive and performative, approaches absorbed from the world of fine art and assimilated into the working philosophy of many contemporary ceramic artists. The paradox lies in the fact that artists such as these are pushing at the boundaries of ceramic convention. It's new ground they are uncovering, but they are doing it with ancient ground, literally mud. And in many cases they are choosing to make their work with the earliest tools – their own hands. Eschewing traditional processes of production, decoration and permanence, they are delighting in the qualities of unadorned clay.

Of course not all contemporary ceramic artists make transitory or installation work, and the hand-formed, fired clay object is still very much alive and kicking. In many cases these objects are not straightforward in their process or material qualities and are somewhat defined by their staging or context. Anne Mercedes, for example, makes abstract compositions in which the kiln is a welcome disrupter. Her use of materials that are likely to warp is an attempt to orchestrate the upheavals firing can bring.

Kerry Jameson is another artist who has worked with the rubble of failed firings. Her figures are given physical form by a range of working methods such as 'mending' these fragments, or combining modelled earthenware with other materials – found

LEFT: Phoebe Cummings, *Flora*, detail from residency studio, Victoria and Albert Museum, London, 2010. Raw clay. *Photo: Sylvain Deleu.*

Sculpting and handbuilding

objects, organic matter, fabric and fibre. Jameson sees her work as creating an environment (a material world) that gives rise to an emotional world. Influenced by medieval painting, amongst other things, her complex narratives are executed with a purposeful simplicity evoking a provocative dialogue.

Turner Prize winner Grayson Perry has done much to challenge the apathetic among us that ceramics isn't all innate amateurism, domesticity and benign craftiness. Rather brilliantly, he has done so by embodying these notions in his work, whilst simultaneously blowing them apart. Perry has adopted a universal and agreeable form for his handbuilt pots; he speaks of pots and pottery, and all his pieces are coil-built. But a closer look at his work reveals an anarchic world of heavily-layered imagery and confrontational themes – social mores, autobiography, pornography, transvestism and the adventures of Alan Measles, the artist's teddy bear, among them.

Cynthia Lahti is an artist based in Portland, Oregon, USA. Her practice is diverse and her use of materials inquisitive. Currently she works with ceramic materials and paper, and produces sculptures, drawings and collage. 'I maintain a very intense studio practice of drawing and creating mixed-media pieces. They often inspire the sculptural work but are also works of art unto themselves. All of my artistic practices feed off of each other but I feel that the sculptures are influenced the most by the drawings and collages.'

Cynthia Lahti, *Braid*, 2011. Soda-fired ceramic, 36 x 20 x 20 cm (14 x 7¾ x 7¾ in). *Photo: courtesy of the artist.*

Contemporary approaches

Cynthia Lahti, *Vault Alarm*, 2010. 15 sculptures arranged on a wooden table. Raku, salt high fire, reduction high fire, 130 x 79 x 97 cm (51 x 31 x 38 in). *Photo: courtesy of the artist.*

Lahti's work demonstrates the symbiotic nature of a mixed-media practice. It's also clear that she is enamored with her materials and the possibilities offered by the ceramic process – letting the clay speak for itself and giving her sculptures up to happenstance. 'I sculpt the ceramic pieces using the additive method. I will often need to build armatures of wire and crinkled paper to help support them as them are being made. The actual sculpting is very focused and intense. When it is leatherhard I can remove the armature and paper and hollow it out. After they are bisque-fired, I may add a surface treatment to the piece in the form of glazes, stains or slips. Often I will leave the clay surface unaltered and just let the firings manipulate the clay body. I welcome accidents and the like, the unpredictable nature of firings. I have been very excited by my result in cone 10 reduction firings, especially soda and salt firings, but also love the surfaces of raku and pit firings.'

Ruan Hoffmann is a multi-disciplinary artist based in South Africa. His ceramic output consists primarily of 'thrown' plates emblazoned with graphic images and hand-rendered type. Hoffmann makes round slabs by throwing a ball of clay at an angle onto a canvas-covered surface until it is thin and relatively even. He then drapes it over a mould to make it ever so slightly concave. Hoffman's plates resemble pages from a journal, containing personal commentary and recordings on diverse subjects from Internet scammers and flora and fauna to politics and personal events. They are pithy, doom-laden, irreverent,

115

Sculpting and handbuilding

Ruan Hoffmann, *Much Love Me* (detail), 2011. Installation of 100 ceramic plates. *Photo: Xylem and Phloem.*

abrasive and jewel-like. Recurring motifs include a delicate and repetitive thin blue line, conjuring an image of the artist painstakingly drawing with quill and ink on curling paper, Tom Phillips-esqe, word maps and word searches, and various incarnations of tear drops. Viewed individually, they are delicate, with gold lustre, decals, washes and fine drawing. The gently-cupped forms and snippets of text are oddly reminiscent of reminders or 'notes to self' scribed in the palm of a hand. Encountered en masse, as Hoffmann often presents them, they are a tender and beguiling evocation of the frantic, cascading, flickering channel-hopping of 21st century on-screen life.

A recent development, which is in contrast to the highly-coloured canvases of Hoffmann's plates, is a series of funerary vases and canopic-style jars. Hoffmann describes these as 'soiled, abject and anti-ceramic'. They are bulbous, asymmetric and beautifully odd – a result of the free-form building process. The vases are lidless and look headless, maybe because the forms are so human. The canopic jars are dark surfaced and sinister, with pools of glass in the eye recesses.

British Ceramics Biennial 2011 award-winner **Phoebe Cummings** completed an MA in Ceramics and Glass at the Royal College of Art in 2005. Her work explores the possibilities of clay as a raw material. Disregarding notions of ceramics as a studio-based practice, and ceramic objects as permanent possessions, her sculptural works and installations are constructed directly on site as temporary interventions, where they may be left to disintegrate or be broken down after a set time, and the material collected and re-made as new works within new locations. (See image on p.112.)

Contemporary approaches

ABOVE: Ruan Hoffmann, *Funerary Vases*, 2012. Various free-form coiled vases including two canopic style jars, height: approx. 70–80 cm (27½ x 31½ in). *Photo: Mari Engelbreght.*

RIGHT: Phoebe Cummings, view of residency studio, Victoria and Albert Museum, London, 2012. Raw clay. *Photo: Sylvain Deleu.*

Sculpting and handbuilding

Lilly Zuckerman, series of pinched vessels on wooden table (detail), 2010. Earthenware and pine. *Photo: Cody Goddard.*

The intensive labour of construction is heightened by the work's temporary existence, playing on expectations both of objects and material, where pieces remain only as a photograph or memory. Cummings' painstaking process involves hand-modelling alongside various texture-producing methods – for example, in *Production Line*, 2011, a solid base of clay was covered over with clay squeezed through a tea strainer.

Embedded in the work is a sense of time and its shifting scales, referencing the prehistoric formation of the material itself, the visible manifestations of time as traced by the making processes and the relatively brief existence of the piece. However intricate and detailed the works may be, they can always be reduced in essence to mud, and in this way clay operates as an infinite matter through which ideas are formed.

Manuel Canu's work is concerned with the process of acculturation – the cultural and psychological change that results when cultures collide. Having lived, studied and worked away from his native Italy for some time, an experience that forced him to consider the meaning of home, Canu's work developed into an exploration of traditions, cultures and beliefs, specifically as seen through the prism of architecture. Canu sees architecture as a meeting ground between the old and the new, and a mirror to the cultures it serves.

Canu works with raw clay in situ, responding to the built environment, and fired, glazed, ornamental ceramics. The structure and substance of a place have a direct relationship on his installations and interventions in clay: 'The installation space itself becomes a primary source of inspiration. I like knowing the story of the place I will be working in: when it was built, for whom and for what purpose, and when possible I find someone to tell me an interesting story about that place.'

Canu handbuilds with raw clay. His installations make use of the plasticity and energy of the clay, and allow for free and spontaneous modelling. By leaving the clay unfired, he preserves some of the marks collected during making, the subtlety and qualities of which would otherwise be lost in the firing process. He seeks out patterns carved in doorframes, old plasterwork on ceilings, window frames and radiators – rolled clay slabs are pressed and coaxed onto and around these features, leaving an imprint in the clay surface. The clay slabs are then formed into decorative ornaments and attached to furniture, walls and floors by pressing them into place. Once complete and left to dry, cracks appear in the clay and the installation gradually dissolves. Canu then recycles the clay for his next project.

Canu works primarily with ordinary red and white clay, which contains a small percentage of 2mm fine grog, relying on high clay plasticity or fat clay, the properties of which help him to easily form the material, avoiding the collapse of the clay body when it is pulled and bent. An extruder is used to produce ropes of clay. The extruder's dies, used for forming the clay, are designed as desired and cut into wood or metal plates. Canu also textures his slabs by drawing into them with the use of various tools like wooden knives, combs and pencils.

Manuel Canu, *Floor installation*, 2011. Unfired red clay, porcelain slip, 3.5 x 1.5 m (11½ x 5 ft). Photo: Ole Akhøj.

Sculpting and handbuilding

Ted Vogel calls himself a collector of objects and a maker of spare parts. His mixed-media approach is demonstrated in his bird and stump sculptures, in which he uses a combination of building methods. This body of work stems from a chance discovery in a Texas cemetery and is permeated with Vogel's love of birds and the natural world.

'My connection for using the tree stump in my art-making vocabulary came to me quite by accident. While driving through a rural town in northern Texas, I discovered a number of carved stone tree-trunk grave markers in the local cemetery. Each is carved in a unique style and includes the symbolic imagery of books (probably the Bible), flowers, axes, vines, branches and birds and ranged in size from a few feet to about eight feet in height. The name and date of the deceased was carved into the bark of the tree or engraved on a scroll that was hung from a severed branch by rope. Through my research, I learned that these memorials where given to members of the fraternal organisation of Woodsman of the World from the late 1800s to around 1920.

'From an early age, I had a passion for the natural world and was intrigued by birds: their wildness, sense of freedom and ability to fly and migrate to mysterious lands. I loved my grandmother's colourfully glazed collection of kitsch ceramic birds that she kept in her sunroom china cabinet, and was amazed to find images of caged birds hanging outside of rustic sod homes built on the Great Plains. Here the canary represented the domestic ideals that families long dreamed of attaining. The canary's beautiful song and brilliant color became a welcome companion for the hard-working women isolated on the American frontier. There is much in art and literature that explores the lore and mythical nature of the bird. Many cultures believe that birds ward off evil, offering protection from harm and bringing renewal of life as they return each spring. In my work, I view birds as guardians or sentinels, similar to the way that biologists regard songbirds to be an important sign of the vitality of local ecosystems, or as early day miners used caged canaries to check the safety of the air.'

Ted Vogel, *Campfire Stories*, 2006–9. Earthenware, black clay, porcelain, wood branches, installation. *Photo: Dan Kvitka.*

Katharine Morling, *Cut (chainsaw)*, 2011. Earth stone, porcelain slip, porcelain and black stain, slab and handbuilding, 47 x 95 x 27 cm (18½ x 37½ x 10½ in). *Photo: Stephen Brayne.*

Vogel's forms are made using several handbuilding techniques. The birds are formed by using simple pinching methods with porcelain or earthenware clays and the stumps are slab-built with earthenware. He then uses press-moulds and carving tools to create a bark-like surface. The images of Vogel's fingerprints are transferred from large digital prints and carved into the surface of the stump. The stumps are fired to 1100°C (2012°F), often using a simple black copper-based glaze or an iron-based terra sigillata.

Katharine Morling's sculptures and installations are beguiling. Exhibiting the appearance and characteristics of torn, cut and curling paper, and contingent on the distinctive black line, drawing is a palpable part of her practice.

Driven by an emotional response to a personal narrative, Morling works in an instinctive way, with one piece leading to the next. She produces small-scale domestic objects and large-scale pieces, each a drawing in three dimensions. Many pieces consist of several components, are arranged to make a tableau staging the still lives of everyday objects.

Morling starts the making process by producing small clay maquettes to help her explore the form and composition; she then makes clay blanks on which to sketch the detail. Working with a range of clays, including porcelain and crank, Morling employs various handbuilding techniques, particularly slab-building. The one constant is the drawn line of black stain. This is fired in, rather than painted on, as is often assumed.

Notes
[1] Anne Mercedes in *Breaking the Mould, New Approaches to Ceramics*, Black Dog Publishing, London, 2007.
[2] Clare Twomey in *Breaking the Mould, New Approaches to Ceramics*, Black Dog Publishing, London, 2007.

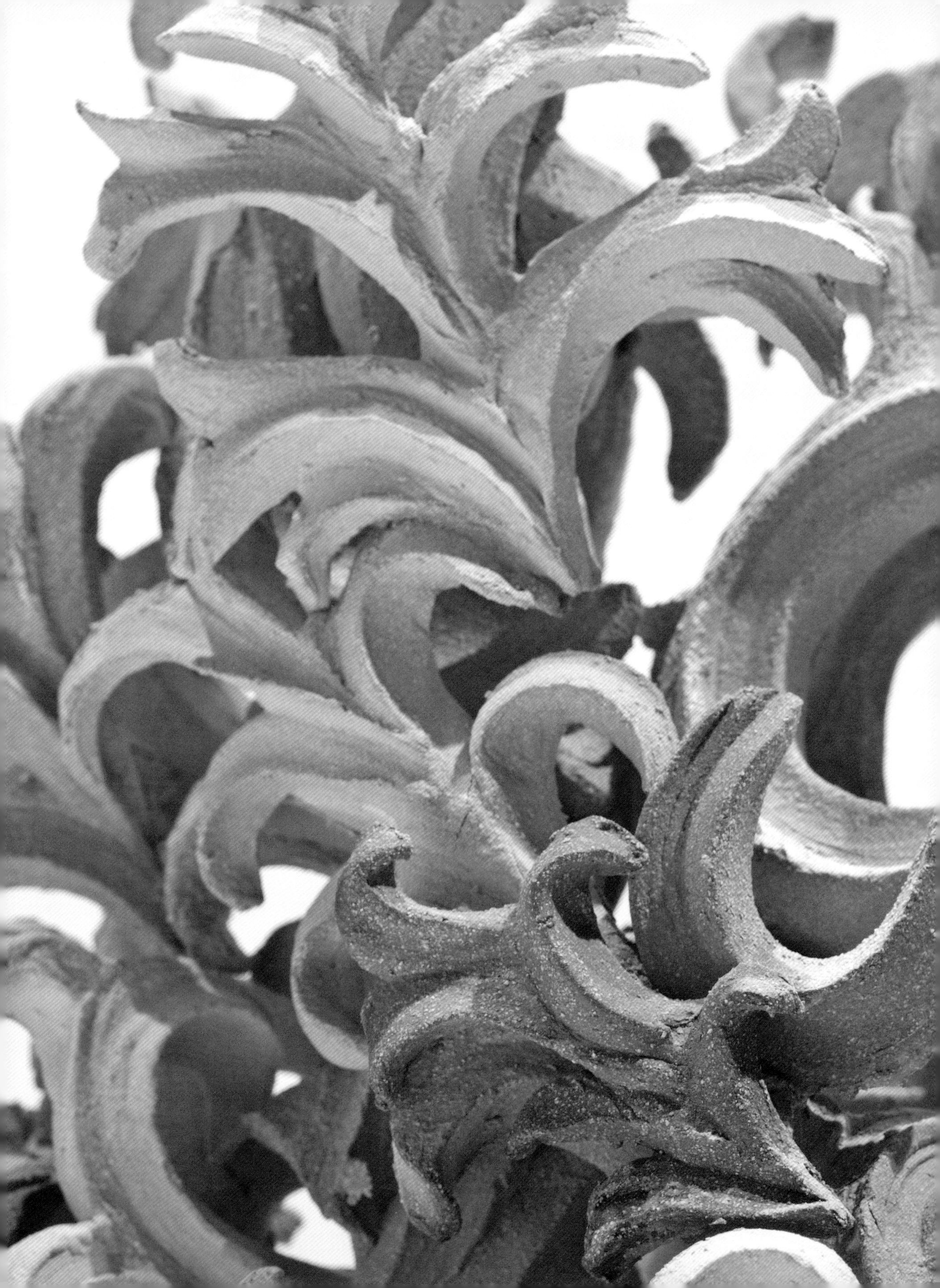

Conclusion

The case studies throughout this book serve to illustrate just some of what is achievable with handbuilding methods. Hopefully they will prompt you to explore the possibilities for yourself. There is plenty of potential for great innovation and expression. The wonderful thing about working with ceramic materials is that it is surprisingly easy to find yourself in new, unchartered territory. When you develop a body of work, you quickly realise that the materials and processes used in conjunction – clay body, additives, building process, scale, surface, application processes, glaze, firing cycle – apart from all the elements of artistry, are often particular to you; in many ways you are on your own. While there is much to be learnt from tradition, history and other ceramicists, there is a unique excitement in creating your own personal alchemy.

LEFT: Jo Taylor, *Large Blue Form* (detail), 2012. Stoneware, height: 70 cm (27½ in). *Photo: Andy Rose.*

RIGHT: Makiko Hastings, letter stamp tool. *Photo: Makiko Hastings.*

Featured Artists

Ingrid Bathe, USA, ingridbathe.com
Stephen Bird, UK/Australia, stephenbird.net
Hans Borgonjon, UK, hansborgonjon.co.uk
Kyra Cane, UK, kyracane.blogspot.com
Manuel Canu, Denmark, manuelcanu.com
Jonathan Cross, USA, jcrosscactus.wordpress.com
Phoebe Cummings, UK, phoebe.cummings@network.rca.ac.ukw
Fenella Elms, UK, fenellaelms.com
Lucy Foakes, UK, lucyfoakes.com
Edith Garcia, UK/USA, edithgarcia.com
Keith Harrison, UK
Makiko Hastings, UK, makikohastings.blogspot.co.uk
David Hicks, USA, dh-studio.com
Ruan Hoffmann, South Africa, ruanhoffmann.com
Amy Jane Hughes, UK, amyjanehughes.com
Kerry Jameson, UK, kerryjameson.com
Christy Keeney, Ireland, christykeeney.co.uk
Nathalie Khayat, Beirut, nathaliekhayat.com
Maria Kristofersson, Sweden, mariakristofersson.se
Cynthia Lahti, USA, cynthialahti.blogspot.com
Jacqueline Leighton Boyce, UK, jacquelineleightonboyce.co.uk
Frankie Locke, UK, frankielocke.co.uk
Claire Loder, UK, claireloder.co.uk
Hanne Mannheimer, UK, hannemannheimer.com
Anne Mercedes, UK, anne-mercedes.com
Katharine Morling, UK, katharinemorling.co.uk
Susan O'Byrne, UK, susanobyrne.com
James Oughtibridge, UK, jamesoughtibridge.co.uk
Sarah Purvey, UK, sarahpurveyceramics.com
Stephanie Quayle, UK, stephaniequayle.co.uk
Consuelo Seixas Radclyffe, UK, consueloradclyffe.com

Merete Rasmussen, UK, mtereterasmussen.com
Aneta Regel, UK, anetaregel.com
Emma Rodgers, UK, emmarodgers.co.uk
Elke Sada, Germany, elkesada.de
Bonnie Smith, USA, bonniemariesmith.com
Jenny Southam, UK, jennysoutham.co.uk
Lisa Stockham, UK, lisastockham.co.uk
Kaori Tatebayashi, UK, kaoriceramics.com
Jo Taylor, UK, jotaylorceramics.com
Rebecca Vernon, UK, rebeccavernon.co.uk
Ted Vogel, USA, accessceramics.org/results/artist/1/
Sophie Woodrow, UK, sophiewoodrow.co.uk
Lily Zuckerman, UK, lillyzuckerman.com

Bibliography

Blandino Betty, *Coiled pottery traditional and contemporary ways*, A&C Black 1984

Bloomfield Linda, *The New Ceramics, Colour in glazes*, A&C Black 2012

Bosworth Joy, *Ceramics with Mixed Media*, A&C Black 2006

Jones Jeffrey, *Studio Pottery in Britain 1900-2005*, A&C Black 2007

De Waal Edmund, *The Pot Book*, Phaidon, 2011

Cooper Emmanuel, *Contemporary Ceramics*, Thames & Hudson, 2009

Cooper Emmanuel, *A History of World Pottery*, BT Batsford, London, 1988
  Breaking the Mould new approaches to ceramics, Black Dog Publishing, 2007

Mattison Steve, *The Complete Potter*, Apple, 2003

Scott Paul, *Painted Clay – Graphic Arts and the Ceramic Surface*, A&C Black 2000

Bliss Gill, *The Potter's Question and Answer Book: 100s of Your Top Questions with 100s of Practical Solutions*, A&C Black, 1999

European Ceramic Work Centre, *The Ceramic Process*, A&C Black, 2005

Further reading

Hooson Duncan & Quinn Anthony, *The Workshop Guide to Ceramics*, Thames and Hudson, 2012

Tristram Fran, *Single Firing, The Pros and Cons*, A&C Black, 1996

LEFT: Ted Vogel, *Campfire Stories – Stump*, 2006–2009. Earthenware, 71 x 71 x 28 cm (27 x 27 x 11 in). *Photo: Dan Kvitka.*

RIGHT: Nathalie Khayat, *Premature Blossoms* 1, 2, 3 & 4. Unglazed porcelain, left to right, ht: 95 cm (37½ in), 125 cm (49¼ in), 120 cm (47¼ in), 80 cm (31½ in). *Photo: Elie Bekhazi.*

Suppliers

UK

Bath Potters' Supplies
Unit 18, Fourth Avenue, Westfield
Trading Estate, Radstock, Nr Bath
BA3 4XE
01761 411077
bathpotters.co.uk

Ceramatech
Units 16 &17 Frontier Works,
33 Queen Street, Tottenham North,
London N17 8JA
0208 885 4492
ceramatech.co.uk

CTM Potters Supplies
Unit 8, Broomhouse Lane Ind Estate,
Edlington, Doncaster, DN12 1EQ
01709 770801

Unit 10A, Mill Park Industrial Estate
White Cross Road, Woodbury
Salterton, EX5 1EL
01395 233077
ctmpotterssupplies.co.uk

Pottery Crafts
Campbell Road, Stoke-on-
Trent, Staffordshire ST4 4ET
01782 745000
potterycrafts.co.uk

Scarva
Unit 20 Scarva Road Industrial
Estate, Scarva Road, Banbridge,
Co Down BT32 3QD
028 40669700
scarva.com

Top Pot Supplies
Barnfield, Fulford Road, Fulford,
Staffordshire ST11 9QT
01782 395825
toppotsupplies.co.uk

USA

Amaco
6060 Guion Road,
Indianapolis,
IN 46254-1222
317 244 6871
amaco.com

Bailey Ceramic Supplies
62-68 Tenbroeck Avenue, Kingston,
New York 12401
845 339 3721
baileypottery.com

Brackers Good Earth Clays
1831 E 1450 Rd, Lawrence,
KS 66044
888 822 1982
brackers.com

Clay Planet
1775 Russell Ave. Santa Clara,
CA 95054
800 443 2529
clay-planet.com

Columbus Clay Company
1080 Chambers Road, Columbus,
Ohio 43212
866 410 2529
columbusclay.com

Creative Clay
5704D General Washington Drive,
Alexandria,
VA 22312.
703-750-9437
creativeclaypottery.com

Hammill & Gillespie
466 Southern Blvd, Washington
Building, Chatham, NJ 07928
800-454-8846
hamgil.com

Laguna Clay Co
14400 Lomitas Avenue,
City of Industry, CA 91746
800 452 4862
lagunaclay.com

Minnesota Clay Co
2960 Niagara Ln, Plymouth,
MN 55447
800 252 9872
mnclay.com

Index

Achaintre, Caroline 100
additions to clay 39, 100
air pockets 13
agateware 82
armatures 39, 41, 115
armature wire 39
Auld, Ian 26

Baldwin, Gordon 26
banding wheel 18, 24, 64, 66, 74
bare clay 77
Bathe, Ingrid 19, 67, 68
Bird, Stephen 54, 87, 89
bone china 100
Borgonjon, Hans 103, 104
breakages 44
building techniques
    combining 99
    supporting 39
burnishing 79

canopic jars 59, 72, 116
Cane, Kyra 52
Canu, Manuel 56, 118, 119
carving 13, 34, 35, 38, 68, 73, 74
carving tips 36
casting slip 81
ceramic pencils 83
Chagall, Marc 65
cheese wire 17
Church, Shay 113
clay blanks 121
clay
    additions to 100
    choosing type 43
    combining 99, 103
    dust 45
    preparation 13, 18
    sketches 50
    working with 43
coiling 9, 13, 23, 24, 26, 42, 56, 72, 73, 84 93, 96, 103
    tips 23
coiled vessels 66, 74
collage 100
coloured slip 81

Coper, Hans 65
crackle slip 81

cracks 44
crank 36
crayons 83
crockery 100, 108
cross-hatching 32, 28, 80
Cross, Jonathan 38
Cummings, Phoebe 112, 116
cuniform script 77

Daintry, Natasha 63
decals 59, 84, 116
decoration 77
De Waal, Edmund 63
digital prints 121
digital tools 59
doodling 58
drawing 47, 51, 52, 54, 56, 58, 84, 107
drying 35, 43, 44, 99
Duckworth, Ruth 26

earthenware 43, 103
Elms, Fenella 87, 94, 96
Engobes 81
equipment 17, 18
extruding 24, 96, 119

firing 44
    reduction 68
firing temperature 43
firing cycles 44
Foakes, Lucy 59, 72, 73
foot ring 64
force drying 44
former 31, 32, 104
found objects 90, 103, 106, 107
Frey, Viola 41
fumes 39
functional ware 64, 65

Garcia, Edith 110
glaze 44, 79, 82, 84, 96, 121
glaze for food use 64
glaze mixing 45
Goldsworthy, Andrew 87

grogged clay 23, 39, 44, 94

Harrison, Keith 56
Hastings, Makiko 58
health and safety 45
Henderson, Ewen 100
Hicks, David 47, 96
Hoffmann, Ruan 115, 116
hollow form – step by step 20
Hughes, Amy Jane 70
Huntley, Brendan 87

Ikemura, Leiko 87
impressing 26, 79, 93
incising 35, 79, 80, 81, 93
inspiration 47
inlaying 79, 80
installation 110, 119

Jameson, Kerry 113, 114
joining slabs 32

Keeny, Christy 89
Khayat, Nathalie 68, 69, 70
kidney – metal and rubber 17
kiln
    lifting work in and out 32
    packing 44
kneading 14, 16, 24
Kristalova, Klara 87
Kristofersson, Maria 56

Lahti, Cynthia, 47, 114, 115
laminated sculpture 36
Leach, Bernard 65
lead-free glaze 64
leatherhard clay 26, 28, 32
Leighton Boyce, Jacqueline 84, 85
Li, Philip 113
Locke, Frankie 36, 38
Loder Claire 90
Long, Richard 87
Lowndes, Gillian 26, 99

Mannheimer, Hanne 106, 107
material, added post-firing 101

Sculpting and handbuilding

Mattison, Steve 9
maquettes 50, 121
Mercedes, Anne 100, 113
mixed media 104, 108, 110, 114, 115, 120
mixing glazes 45, 83
models 50
modelling 30, 108, 118
Mohwald, Gertraud 100
moisture levels 36
moulds 13, 31, 33, 104, 115
Morling, Katharine 121

newspaper 32, 44
Nichrome wire 39
non-toxic glaze 64

O'Byrne, Susan 39
online inspiration 60
once-fired 74
organic matter 101, 114
Oughtibridge, James 33, 34
oxides 34, 79, 82, 93, 104

packing (a kiln) 44
paperclay 39, 41, 43, 68, 104
paper templates 36
performative work 56
Perry, Grayson 114
Phillips, Tom 116
photography 52, 61, 118
plaster bat 16, 18, 24
plaster moulds 33, 72
plastic 44
Picasso, Pablo 65, 89
pinching 9, 19, 24, 26, 68, 73, 96, 103, 121
pinch pot 13, 20, 63, 99
porcelain 23, 36, 43, 68 70, 73, 94, 100, 103
potter's knife 17
potter's needle 17
press moulds 31, 70, 72, 87, 103, 121
Purvey, Sarah 74, 81
pyrometric cones 44

Quayle, Stephanie 94
Quinn, Antony 13

Radclyffe, Consuelo Sexias 104, 106
raku 43
Rasmussen, Merete 24, 26
raw clay 83, 113, 116, 119
    painting on 87
reclaiming clay 13, 16, 18, 33
recording results 44
reduction firing 68
research 47
resists 81
Regel Deleu, Aneta 101
relief 35, 80
Rie, Lucie 65
ritual figures 9
Rodgers, Emma 107, 108, 110
rolling pin 17, 31
Roulette 79

Sada, Elke 51
saggar 36, 45
Scott, Paul 77, 84
Sevres 70
Stockham, Lisa 70, 72
sculpting 13, 38, 108
    tips 39
sgraffito 35, 81
shrinkage 44, 101
single-fired 90
sketchbooks 51, 52, 58
sketching 54, 107, 108
slab box, making of 28
slab-building 9, 13, 26, 72, 70, 89, 90, 91, 96, 108, 121
slab building
    making a slab 26
    with leatherhard clay 28
    soft slab construction 26, 30
    tips 32
slab roller 26
slip 74, 81 84, 93, 94, 80
    coloured 81
Smith, Bonnie Marie 41, 103
social media 60
solid block sculpture 20, 35, 36, 41, 99, 101, 103
Southam, Jenny 34, 50, 58,93
sprigging 80

stains 34, 82, 104, 121
stamps (handmade) 79
stencils 81
stoneware 24, 43
Stockham, Lisa 72
surface
    development 44
    and context 78
    treatments 77, 78, 115

Tatebayashi, Kaori 91
Taylor, Jo 42, 43, 52
temporary interventions 116
terracotta 84, 96, 100
terra sigillata 81, 121
test tiles 44
texture 26, 31, 70, 72, 79, 96, 118
T-material 43
tools 17, 18, 34, 35, 36, 79, 119
throwing 13, 26, 115
Twomey, Clare 113

underglaze 34, 83, 84
unfired clay 113

ventilation 39
Vernon, Rebecca 73, 74
Vessel
    coiling 24
    slab built 67
    pinched and sculpted 67
Vessels 20, 63, 65, 56, 68, 74
Vogel, Ted 120, 121

wall pieces 96, 104, 110
warping 108, 113
wedging 13, 14, 16, 24
Wedgewood 80
wire 104, 108
    that withstands firing 39, 100
wire harp 26
Woodrow, Sophie 93
working environment 48
work station 17
wrapping work 36, 43, 44

Zuckerman, Lily 19, 20, 22, 50, 68, 118